W9-CCS-302

The
Greenhouse
Cookbook

The
Greenhouse
Cookbook

Plant-Based Eating and DIY Juicing

Emma Knight

with Hana James, Deeva Green and Lee Reitelman

Photography by Elena Mari and Nathan Legiehn

PENGUIN

an imprint of Penguin Canada, a division of Penguin Random House Canada Limited

Canada • USA • UK • Ireland • Australia • New Zealand • India • South Africa • China

First published 2017

Copyright © 2017 by Greenhouse Juice Company

All rights reserved. Without limiting the rights under copyright reserved above, no part of this publication may be reproduced, stored in or introduced into a retrieval system, or transmitted in any form or by any means (electronic, mechanical, photocopying, recording or otherwise), without the prior written permission of both the copyright owner and the above publisher of this book.

www.penguinrandomhouse.ca

LIBRARY AND ARCHIVES CANADA CATALOGUING IN PUBLICATION

Knight, Emma L., author

The Greenhouse cookbook : plant-based eating and DIY juicing / Emma Knight ; with Hana James, Deeva Green and Lee Reitelman.

ISBN 978-0-14-319828-4 (paperback)
ISBN 978-0-14-319829-1 (electronic)

1. Fruit juices. 2. Vegetable juices. 3. Vegetarian cooking.
4. Vegetarianism. 5. Cookbooks. I. Title.

TX815.K65 2017   641.87'5   2016-904755-5

Book design by Sarah Dobson and Lisa Jager

Cover design by Rachel Cooper

Cover images by Elena Mari and Nathan Legiehn

Photography, food and prop styling by Elena Mari and Nathan Legiehn

Illustrations by Elena Mari

Printed and bound in China

10 9 8 7 6 5 4 3 2 1

Penguin
Random House
Canada

To our regulars.

Contents

Introduction / 1

About This Book / 9

On DIY Juicing and Plant-Based Eating / 13

Smoothies, Nut Milks and Tonics / 17

A Word About Antioxidants, Fibre and Sugar / 19

Plant Pantry / 22

Breakfasts

Dark Cherry Berry Smoothie Bowl / 31

Peach Crisp Smoothie Bowl / 32

Overnight Oats / 35

Quinoa Banana Pancakes / 36

Cashew "Yogurt" / 39

Warming Winter Oatmeal with Roasted Chestnut Purée / 40

Vanilla Bean Chia Pudding / 42

Spiced Grain-Free Granola with Brazil Nut Fibre / 45

Ancient Grain, Seed and Nut Loaf / 46

Chocolate Hazelnut Spread / 49

Avocado Toast with Harissa and Sprouts / 50

Moroccan Sweet Potato Hash / 53

Lunches and Dinners

Pea Shoot and Asparagus Salad with Toasted Hazelnuts / 57

Kale Salad with Roasted Beets and Avocado / 58

Broccoli Soup with Sweet Potato Croutons / 61

Tuscan White Bean Soup with Dinosaur Kale / 65

Socca with Walnut Pesto and Arugula / 66

Quinoa Pilaf "Chicoutimi" with Peas, Napa Cabbage and Mint / 69

Spaghetti Squash with Ginger, Chili, Lime and Grilled Tofu / 70

Miso-Glazed Eggplant, Kabocha Squash and Black Rice / 73

Summer Ratatouille with Creamy Polenta / 74

Spicy Mushroom Tacos with Crispy Tempeh / 77

Lentils and Brown Rice with Rainbow Chard, Roasted Carrots and Tahini / 79

Spiralized Zucchini Mac and Cheese with Oat Crumb Crust / 83

Soba Noodles in Miso Broth with Daikon, Mushrooms and Crispy Tofu / 85

Very Veggie Curry with Exploded Yellow Lentils / 87

Amaranth-Stuffed Vine Leaves and Fava Purée with Onion Condiment / 91

Bites

Warm Beet Hummus / 99

Roasted Eggplant Dip / 100

Sundried Tomato Tapenade / 103

Raw Carrot Chipotle Dip / 104

Scottish Oatcakes / 107

Flax Crackers with Black Olives / 108

Preserved Rainbow Peppers / 111

Hot, Crispy Chickpeas / 112

Baked Brassica Bites / 115

Za'atar Kale Chips / 116

Chia Seed Chai Energy Bars / 119

Naked Almonds / 120

Blueberry Lemon Bites / 123

Double Cacao Protein Bites / 123

Desserts

Vanilla Bean Cheesecake with Coconut Whipped Cream / 127
Raspberry Tart with Pistachio Crust / 128
Oatmeal Chocolate Chip Sea Salt Cookies / 131
Fall Fruit Crumble / 132
Raw Dark Chocolate Bars with Fig Base / 135
Apple Pecan Squares with Caramel Sauce / 136
Sweet Potato Brownies / 139
Pumpkin Pie with Coconut Whipped Cream / 140
Sticky Ginger Cake with Lemon Sauce / 143
Key Lime Cups / 144
Chocolate Hemp Peanut Butter Balls / 147

Juices

Equipment / 150
The Good / 153
East of Eden / 154
Gold Rush / 157
Wake Up / 158
Deep Roots / 161
Rabbit, Run / 162
The Giver / 165
The Misfit / 166
Cabbages and Kings / 169
Oz / 170
Harlequin / 173
Boom / 174
Ophelia / 177
Alpha / 178
TKO / 181
8½ / 182
Juice Cocktails / 184

Smoothies

Rococoa / 189
Rio Deal / 190
Picante Green / 193
Leo / 194
Berry Eclectic / 197
Jobim / 198
Firefly / 201
Sweet Potato Chai / 202
Radio / 205
Black Seed / 206
Wild Oats / 209
Pistachio, Cardamom and Rose Water
Lassi / 210
Mint and Black Pepper Savoury Lassi / 213

Nut Milks

Soaking Nuts / 216
Almond Milk / 219
Cashew Milk / 220
Combo Nut and Seed Milk / 223
Brazil Nut Milk / 224
Smoothie Milk / 227
Pink Milk / 228
Green Milk / 231
Harvest Milk / 232
Choco-Maca-Milk / 235
Matcha Ginger Milk / 236
Coconut Milk / 239
Piloto / 241
Cold-Brew Coffee / 242
Chai Concentrate / 243
Almond Chai / 245

Tonics

Chia Seed Hydrator / 249
Clean-Zing / 250
Hydra / 253
Teresa's Ginger Drink / 254
YYZ / 257
Beet Kvass / 258
Nettle Switchel / 261
Healing Vegetable Broth / 263

Cleanses

What Is a Cleanse? / 266
Cleanse FAQs / 269
Pre- and Post-Cleanse Menus / 272
Gentle Cleanse / 275
Standard Cleanse / 276
Green Cleanse / 279

Acknowledgements / 280
References / 282
Index / 286

Introduction

It was close to midnight. The temperature had dipped below minus 40, and not for the first time that week. Inside a one-room cottage in a peaceful Toronto neighbourhood, Bob Marley and the Wailers competed with the mechanical din of hydraulic presses.

In one corner, a man in a chef's coat was dropping scrubbed, trimmed beets down a steel chute and into the heart of the largest machine, where they were ground and then pressed between two metal plates. The shop was filled with their sweet, earthy smell.

Along counters around the room, young men and women were working elbow to elbow. One was straining blended almonds, dates and vanilla through a muslin cloth. Another was pressing gnarled roots of ginger using a smaller, box-shaped press. I was in the back corner sticking labels onto hot, newly sanitized glass bottles.

So intent were we upon our respective tasks that we did not hear the knocking.

The Wailers wailed, the presses pressed and the pounding on the door intensified until one young woman looked up. The windows were dense with fog. She unlocked the store's front door. There stood a man of about our age, pink-cheeked and slightly wild-eyed in his parka.

"Do you have anything?" he asked without preamble. "I need an East of Eden." He poked his head inside the shop in search of a bottle. "Please," he added. "I have cash."

At this point our little shop had been open for two days.

Our first day, a grim Wednesday in January, an entire night's worth of juice had sold within a few hours. We kept the doors open until sundown, offering colourful samples to those who made the pilgrimage through ice and snow but were too late. When evening fell we spun into production for the next day's double batches and continued until dawn. Thursday morning, within an hour of opening, not a single bottle remained for sale.

Our visitor, it emerged, was a neighbourhood bartender working the late shift. He had happened on us the previous morning and had found our juice to his liking. He was ready for more.

By this time some of us had been awake for nearly three days. The juice—along with the exhilaration of a new venture and the astonishment that people were coming—was keeping us standing. As such, we appreciated the urgency of his plea. We handed him a bottle of liquid emerald. He bowed his thanks and disappeared into the darkness.

———

The "we" of this book is the family of friends behind Greenhouse, a Toronto company specializing in organic, cold-pressed juice. We are a motley band of siblings, couples, best-friend's-little-sisters and so on. We like to think of ourselves as the Arcade Fire of the juice world.

While some of us—namely, Anthony, Sophie and Deeva Green, whose parents Don and Denyse are Greenhouse's North Star—grew up drinking raw vegetable juice, others among us have acquired the taste more recently. At least one of us had to muster a significant amount of sang-froid before that first sip of a liquid that was green without the help of food dye.

But the uninitiated were curious. Otherwise rational people were extolling this habit in such fervent tones (their skin dewy, the whites of their eyes shining with the earnestness of their message) that we had to at least try it. We had to get to the bottom of why our friends had seemingly forgotten about triple-shot lattés with emojis drawn in the foam and were instead clutching bottles of what looked like radioactive swamp water close to their hearts.

We sought it out with ease; our respective careers had taken us to New York and Los Angeles, where shops peddling the stuff had sprung up overnight on every street corner. Without consulting one another, we each crossed the threshold of one of these establishments, chuckled at the seemingly absurd price point and picked one.

Quickly, before we changed our minds, before the smell of kale had a chance to send a signal from our nostrils to our brains ("Abort! Abort! Abort!"), we took a sip.

Right. Huh.

We took another.

Oh. Okay.

We re-examined the label of the specimen in our hands and took a third. Then we downed the thing, impressed with our follow-through, and moved on with our day.

But something was different. There was a certain fire in our bellies that spread to our limbs and made us stride purposefully through our to-do lists without pausing to clear the fog. Curiously, there wasn't any. Our minds felt quietly alert. There was no flutter and no crash. We remained buoyant until the work was done and then were able to settle peacefully, with no residual jumpiness.

If this is all sounding faintly pharmaceutical, consider that many of us were accustomed to having our productivity pegged to a drug—caffeine—that keeps you aloft until it doesn't. What we had discovered was something different. This was energy from vegetables, in a much larger quantity than one would be able to eat in a single sitting; a wave of nutrients that our bodies absorbed efficiently. We felt refreshed, and very alive. The evangelists had not been wrong.

As we began to make a habit of the juice, we noticed other subtle changes in our behaviour. We found ourselves forgetting to have our mid-morning coffee. We were moving more, eating more vegetables and fiddling around with chia seeds. Having discovered that warm lift, we were gravitating toward ways to perpetuate the feeling.

Did becoming born-again juicers cause us to abandon pleasures like buttery croissants, espresso, red wine and skepticism, once and for all? Thankfully, no. But drinking a green juice every day was giving us more energy, helping us to part ways with some of our least endearing habits and strengthening our immune systems.

By the spring of 2013, a collective fantasy had begun to emerge. It took the shape of a beautiful little shop that would serve the highest quality of raw, organic, cold-pressed juice to the Toronto community in simple, reusable glass bottles.

Three of the friends—Anthony Green, Jacob Cohl and Stephen Shaw—had forged their bond in childhood over their mutual appreciation for a sophisticated, three-man piece of equipment known as a water balloon launcher.

In the middle of that spring, a certain storefront became available in Toronto's Summerhill neighbourhood. We all knew the building well: it was a funny little cottage that, in summers past, had housed the neighbourhood ice cream shop. It also backed onto the alleyway from which Anthony, Jacob and Stephen had launched the majority of their formative water balloons. Wouldn't it be fitting, they must have thought to themselves, to launch something else from that location?

They pulled the trigger, so to speak. Anthony and his sister Sophie Green, Jacob and his wife, Sage Scully, and Stephen and his wife, Jessie Tuttle, formed a company whose name was derived from the little building that would become our original shop: "Greenhouse." Another friend, Sarah Dobson, designed a logo, also inspired by the structure.

Not everything about this idea was convenient. Although it was their hometown, Toronto was not where the new partners lived; they were each tied to other cities by their careers, not one of which was remotely related to juice. This problem appeared to be solved when Hana James, Sophie's best friend's little sister, who was living in Toronto and running her own successful healthy food and beverage business called Café Shu, agreed to join her old friends as Greenhouse's co-founder and operating partner.

In the months before launch, the partners built Greenhouse from afar, each contributing in areas that corresponded to their talents. I was the last to get involved; I finished graduate school in Paris late that spring, then joined

Anthony in LA, where I began to assist with branding. Our naïve plan was that, when launch time came, we would all descend on Toronto for two weeks to help Hana get the store open—and she would take it from there.

On December 18, 2013, Anthony and I took the red-eye to Toronto from LA with carry-on bags. We planned to spend the holidays with our families, help to put the finishing touches on the store, participate in the first day or two of operations and then go back to our other lives.

The frigid week in which Greenhouse was born seemed ideal; surely only immediate family members would drink cold juice in such weather, we reasoned. Hana and the handful of young nutritionists she had hired to make and sell the juice would have lots of time to work out any hiccoughs before word got out and demand (we hoped) eventually picked up.

Not so. To our great surprise, from the moment we opened the doors of the tiny cottage that doubled as our production facility and retail shop on January 8, 2014, keeping up with demand meant all hands on deck, all the time. We quickly understood that we had created a 24-hour-a-day, seven-day-a-week operation, that we would need more than one partner on the ground—and that we required more than a 300-square-foot cottage from which to make and sell juice.

More importantly, we began to witness in our early customers the same transformation that we ourselves had experienced. The bartender who visited us on that bleak midwinter night told us that drinking juice rather than caffeine to stay alert through late shifts was helping him manage his anxiety. A local restaurateur divulged that his daily East of Eden (page 154) had caused his gout symptoms to disappear, much to his doctor's amazement. A third customer emailed us to say that drinking our juice had motivated her to make such drastic changes in her caffeine intake, diet, exercise and general lifestyle that she had seen improvements in her cardiovascular health, strength and overall well-being.

While drinking raw vegetable juice is no doubt a good thing in and of itself, the real magic appears to be in the domino effect a juice habit can have on other behaviour patterns, knocking them in a more constructive direction. From our very first days in business we have had the privilege of watching Greenhouse serve as a catalyst for healthy change in people's lives.

It was over two years before Anthony and I made it back to LA to pack up our apartment there. Anthony put his film career on hold to run the young company, and I jumped down the rabbit hole with him and Hana. We lived with Anthony's unbelievably supportive parents and two enormous dogs, and over those first two years we opened seven additional shops, a centralized production facility and a citywide electric-car delivery service.

The prospect of sparking healthy change is also why we're excited about this book. Frequenting our shops is not the only way to give juice a chance (shocking, we know). You can absolutely make your own. The second half of this book, in which we have included all of our juice, smoothie, nut milk and tonic recipes to date (and then some), will hopefully prove that point.

You might just find, as we have, that once you've had your afternoon green juice, you feel like doing a little bit of frolicking, whether that takes the form of leaping around your living room to the Rolling Stones (my mom's preferred form of workout) or something more square like a yoga class.

Then, post-frolic, we wouldn't be surprised if you started to feel a bit peckish. But a particular kind of peckish. Not the kind where there is a voice behind your left ear whispering *ramencookiesicecream* and you need to devour something right now or you'll start breaking things. More like the kind where you want to make and savour a satisfying meal that's good for you. Something that will keep you floating on this cloud that you have lived on ever since that green fairy liquid hit your lips. (Juice, not absinthe, but we'd forgive you for confusing the two.)

To that end, we've also filled this book with simple but outlandishly delicious plant-based food recipes. They are all dairy free and gluten free, which doesn't mean that you can't sandwich them between slices of grilled halloumi or serve them with a hunk of sourdough, if you so choose. It just means you don't have to; they'll be equally satisfying exactly as they're written.

Balance looks different for everyone, and it doesn't stand still. We're always striving for a version of it that lets us live in the moment while looking out for a healthy future. That's what we're trying to achieve with Greenhouse, and that's what we're trying to achieve with this book. That, and to convince you to join the Cult of the Juice.

About This Book

This book was born out of the Greenhouse blog, under the generous guidance of Andrea Magyar at Penguin Random House. While we have striven to give it a unified voice (mine, lucky me—I bribed my way in), its authors are, in fact, multiple.

The juice, smoothie, nut milk and tonic recipes are mostly from the company repertoire. Greenhouse Co-founder Hana James developed a number of these, as did cold-pressed pioneer Jermaine Jonas.

The plant-based food recipes would have been nowhere near as interesting without Deeva Green and Lee Reitelman, a pair of avid and imaginative cooks, who took on the lion's share of recipe creation and testing. Deeva is the youngest sister of Anthony and Sophie Green, and Lee is her partner in life as well as in the kitchen.

When I began working on this book, Deeva and Lee had just returned from a year in Bordeaux, where they were studying agricultural practices, teaching English and charming their way into every possible kitchen to acquire new techniques. My only source of trepidation in bringing them on, expressed in muted tones to Anthony, was Deeva and Lee's strong affinity for capers, which I had observed over the years. "Emma is scared that you're going to put capers in every recipe," Anthony told them in a loud voice at a Green family dinner that night. I tried to deny it, but I'm a bad liar. As a result, there are no capers in this whole book, not even in the Sundried Tomato Tapenade (page 103). This is my fault, and I apologize. If you like a good caper, please scatter them at will.

As you will notice in the recipe headnotes, other dishes in this Greenhouse community potluck have been contributed by our in-house nutritionists Brooke Lundmark and Emily Kreeft; by our dear friends Teresa Ayson, Tara Tomulka, Alan Bekerman and Christine Flynn; and by those people who first taught us to cook and enjoy food: our parents, Doug Knight and Colleen Flood and Don and Denyse Green.

The photographs in this book were styled and shot by Toronto artists Elena Mari and Nathan Legiehn, another in-life-and-in-work duo. Elena was one of our very first store managers at our shop on Macpherson Avenue, and she and Nathan have been helping to define Greenhouse's aesthetic with their stunning art direction and photography—and contributing delicious recipes to our blog (the Pumpkin Pie with Coconut Whipped Cream on page 140 is Elena's)—since our first spring. They are enormous fun to work with, even when bad things happen (we once lost a drone together, but that's another story for another day).

On DIY Juicing and
Plant-Based Eating

While technically you could call us professional juicers (now that we have a juice company and everything), we still prefer to describe our juice-related activities—and those we espouse—with the made-up term, "recreational juicing." We define this approach as drinking juice whenever the mood strikes, because it tastes good, because it makes you feel good and because it's good for you—and not because you're a born-again health fanatic who has sworn off solids and who flosses with kimchi.

Ever since the dawn of the interwebs (or perhaps before), we've been bombarded with colliding messages about what we should and should not ingest. One message has not changed: eat your vegetables.

That vegetables are good for us has been known for quite some time. Drinking liquid recently extracted from said vegetables, for health and even for enjoyment, has been common practice in certain circles for decades. It just hasn't been considered very cool.

But as one of our favourite Bobs has been trying to warn us, the times they are a-changin'.

The young folk are becoming kinfolk. We're weaving hyperlocal sweater vests out of our own facial hair, taking axe-sharpening classes on weekends and collecting fiddleheads in the folds of our unisex skirts.

Hippies have given way to hipsters who, like their predecessors (but in a more ironic way), are prone to such esoteric practices as vegetarianism, veganism, frolicking in muddy fields and juicing.

Juice—especially the cold-pressed kind—has swept the planet in recent years, making peppy young things from Halifax to Hong Kong even peppier and supposedly offering a gem-toned solution to everything that's wrong with us.

Given the speed of contagion, the celebrity endorsements and the high price point, it's easy to dismiss the whole concept as a fad designed to dupe feckless millennials out of our parents' retirement savings. But it isn't. Drinking juice is an efficient way to absorb a lot of nutrients, and we think it's here to stay.

The crazier our schedules get, the harder it becomes to peel, chop and massage all of the vegetables that, in a perfect world, we would like to consume in a day. This is where "DIY Juicing" comes in: while it is not a substitute for eating your vegetables, drinking raw vegetable juices, smoothies and other plant-based drinks is the simplest way we know of to soak up the health benefits from large quantities of raw produce, balancing convenience with wellness and ephemeral pleasure with long-term health. Thus, in this book you'll find 50 of our favourite juice, smoothie, nut milk and tonic recipes, adapted for home use.

You may be getting a sinking feeling that this miraculous liquid is angling to depose dinner. Rest assured—it is not. Juice devotees though we are, we're also strong believers in eating. We do it all the time. Eating is one of the most enjoyable activities on the planet; it should not take a back seat to juicing and feeling smug.

With the more than 50 breakfast, lunch, dinner, snack and dessert recipes in this book, we have sought to demonstrate how easy it is to create delicious and decadent plant-based, gluten-free dishes that even the most avid omnivores will find thrilling. We know this because we are avid omnivores, and we find them thrilling. If your diet is entirely plant based, or if you are sensitive to gluten, dairy or eggs, you can cook any recipe in this book.

If your tastes and tolerances are more eclectic but you would like to eat more plants, more often, consider this book a healthy foundation upon which to build whatever type of lifestyle suits you best. (Or a healthy foundation upon which to rest a hamburger.)

Don't hesitate to embellish. Add sharp slices of pecorino to the Pea Shoot and Asparagus Salad with Toasted Hazelnuts (page 57), pile some buffalo mozzarella on top of your Socca with Walnut Pesto and Arugula (page 66) and use dairy yogurt or kefir in the lassis (pages 210 and 213). Make the Oatmeal Chocolate Chip Sea Salt Cookies (page 131) and Sticky Ginger Cake with Lemon Sauce (page 143) with wheat flour, and spread the Warm Beet Hummus (page 99) and Roasted Eggplant Dip (page 100) on the fluffiest pita you can find.

In other words, our intention is for this book to be filled with simple, delightful possibilities for eaters of all proclivities. We want you to be able to cook from it freely and, in the process, to find new ways to love plants.

Smoothies, Nut Milks and Tonics

Smoothies

A juice is not usually, in and of itself, a satisfying meal. A smoothie, on the other hand, most certainly can be. While a juicer's job is to separate nutrient-dense plant liquid from pulp or insoluble fibre, a smoothie, whipped up in a blender, contains both.

Blenders require liquids in order to function, and so do smoothies. We like to use Smoothie Milk (page 227), a toned-down version of any of our nut or seed milks, for most of our more decadent smoothies. For a lighter touch, try a fresh juice, coconut water or just plain filtered water. If your blender is making low, angry mooing sounds at any point, there might not be enough liquid. Turn it off, shift things around and add more liquid if needed. There should always be enough to fully submerge the blades.

If we're treating a smoothie as a meal, we like to add a big handful of leafy greens and some protein, often in the form of seeds like pumpkin, flax and hemp and/or nuts or nut butters. These also provide healthy, hunger-curbing fats, as do avocados and coconut oil. If we're craving some extra fibre, we'll add a hand-ful of oats or some psyllium seed husks, which contributes greatly to thickness. If we need a boost, we'll add vitamin C–rich camu camu berry or a blue-green alga like spirulina. For tastiness we'll add a few dashes of cinnamon or cacao powder or the seeds of a vanilla bean. A handful of ice cubes, a spin in your trusty blender and voila. Breakfast (or lunch, or whatever) is served.

Nut Milks

Whether you avoid dairy or not, homemade nut milk makes an excellent treat. On its own, warmed up with a shot of espresso, served over ice with deeply infused chai tea or blended into a smoothie, there is no comparison between rich, sat-isfying homemade nut and seed milks and the watery, preservative-filled boxed ones lining grocery shelves. We resort to those when we haven't had time to make our own, but we prefer the fresh stuff whenever possible.

Buy raw, unprocessed nuts and seeds from a reliable source with a reasonably quick turnover (you don't want them to have been sitting, neglected, in the same bulk bin for a decade), and store them in the fridge to keep them fresh for as long as possible. Sort through your nuts before you start and eliminate any that look rotten or mouldy. Raw nut milks are extremely fragile; one bad guy will wreck the whole batch.

Tonics

We define tonics as liquid pick-me-ups that, in most cases, call for less of an investment in time and ingredients—and last much longer in the fridge—than a juice, nut milk or smoothie.

Traditional Chinese medicine places great value on taking tonic plants as preventative medicine and a means of strengthening natural defences. In our minds, a tonic is something that tones our systems, making them more flexible and better able to adapt under pressure without cracking. We know that this makes us sound a bit like the salesmen in movies who hop up on pedestals at fairs to sell dubious remedies in little brown bottles, but we're okay with that.

Some of our tonics, such as Teresa's Ginger Drink (page 254), take a bit longer to prepare and are worth making in big, concentrated batches every two weeks or so, while others, such as Clean-Zing (page 250), take only a minute to whip up and can be done on the fly. One, our Beet Kvass (page 258) is fermented. This may sound daunting—and it's true that fermenting requires caution and patience—but it's not difficult. This tonic is probiotic, meaning that it supports the good bacteria in your gut, which is helpful for digestion, immunity and weight management.

For most of these recipes, you'll need some kind of citrus juicer (the manual kind is perfectly adequate); a source of pure water (our recipes call for filtered water, but you can use any water that tickles your fancy); large, sealable, sterile jars; and occasionally another piece of equipment like a blender, juicer or stovetop.

We call them tonics not because they pair well with gin (though mostly they do, with the possible exception of the Healing Vegetable Broth, page 263), but because of their restorative, invigorating and immunity-boosting properties.

A Word About Antioxidants, Fibre and Sugar

Antioxidants

A natural chemical process called oxidation takes place in our bodies every day. Getting stressed out, drinking lots of alcohol and smoking (three things that tend to go well together) can accelerate oxidation. Disrupting the natural oxidation process can create unstable and potentially destructive molecules called free radicals. If free radical production is left uncontrolled and exceeds your body's protective defences, free radicals can damage your cells. Cell damage caused by free radicals is a suspected factor in many diseases, including cancer, heart disease, Alzheimer's, arthritis and diabetes. Fortunately, we have a natural defence against free radicals: antioxidants.

Antioxidants are molecules that can safely interact with free radicals to intervene in their path of destruction before too much cell damage is done. They come in many different forms: as naturally occurring enzyme systems in the body, as vitamins (such as vitamins C and E), as minerals (such as selenium and manganese) and as plant compounds (such as beta-carotene and lycopene). Many plant foods are good sources of antioxidants. The best way to arm your body with a variety of these molecules is to infuse your diet with plants of all colours.

Fibre

When you run plants through a juicer, you are separating the liquid, which is rich in nutrients (including antioxidants) and is easily assimilated by the body, from the plant solid, which is filled with beneficial insoluble fibre. Insoluble fibre, the bulky kind that does not dissolve in water (as opposed to soluble fibre, which dissolves in water and thus does not get left behind by the juicing process), is important in many ways. We would never advocate living without it. It is necessary for digestion, it gives us a feeling of satiety and it slows down the rate at which the body metabolizes sugars, helping to avoid a roller coaster of insulin peaks and troughs. However, it takes work for the body to break down fibre, and it can therefore get in the way of complete nutrient absorption. When you bypass insoluble fibre with a juice, nutrients are absorbed more easily, but so is sugar; it is worth keeping this in mind when you are drinking juices that include sweet fruits so you can make sure to include plenty of insoluble fibre in your diet in other ways.

Sugar

Many wise people have argued that juice is bad for you because it contains a great deal of sugar and little else. It is true that most of the boxed, bottled, jarred or canned liquids that we're used to calling "juice" have been highly processed to extend their shelf life, reduce the cost of producing them and make them irresistible. These juices contain few of the nutritional properties of the fruits and vegetables from which they derive, but all of the sugar (and often more added on top of that). Raw juices that you make at home from fresh produce, on the other hand, like the cold-pressed juices that we make at Greenhouse, are in another category. There can be naturally occurring sugars in these juices, too, if the recipes call for sweet fruits or vegetables like apples or beets, but the sugars in these juices are accompanied by the nutrients that make them worthwhile.

Plant Pantry

——————

Here's an A–Z list of some of our favourite plants to eat and juice, and a few sentences from our nutritionist friends about what's so darned great about them. Whether you're cooking or juicing (but particularly if you're juicing), we recommend giving your vegetables and fruit a good scrub first, possibly with an organic produce wash, and paying special attention to leafy greens and to tricky places like the bottom crevices of celery stalks. Finally, we believe it is worthwhile to source said plants from local growers who use organic farming methods as often as possible, for health and environmental reasons. At the end of the day, plants are better than no plants.

Almonds

Almonds are rich in polyunsaturated and monounsaturated fats, which are heart healthy, support muscle function and provide slow-release energy that helps to offer long-lasting satiety. They are also high in protein and vitamin E and are a good source of minerals such as magnesium, calcium and copper.

Beets

Beets are a great source of phenolic acids, which have antioxidant properties and have been found to have antibacterial, antiviral and anti-inflammatory effects. Beets also improve blood circulation, which is beneficial for heart health.

Blue-Green Algae

Blue-green algae such as spirulina and E3Live taste like swamp water, but are well worth a moment's nose plugging. Blue-green algae have been found to increase physical and mental energy and to enhance the immune system. They are concentrated, easily absorbed sources of a wide range of nutrients.

Apples

Apples are a good source of vitamin C and of soluble fibres ("soluble" meaning water soluble; they don't get lost in the juicing process), which exert prebiotic effects important for metabolism. Pectin, a soluble fibre found in apples, has been found to improve the intestinal muscles' ability to push waste through the gastrointestinal tract.

Brazil Nuts

Brazil nuts are rich in selenium, a mineral that supports immunity and healing. They also provide a good amount of vitamin E, which helps to maintain healthy skin, and of thiamine, a B-complex vitamin that aids in efficient carbohydrate metabolism and promotes a healthy brain and memory.

Butternut Squash

Like other bright orange vegetables, butternut squash is a rich source of carotenoids, antioxidants that have been found to strengthen immunity, and support healthy vision and skin.

Cacao Powder

Cacao has extremely high antioxidant capacity because of its high polyphenolic content and is noted for its role in maintaining vascular health. Cacao is also rich in dietary fibre, which has been associated with a lower risk of chronic disorders like diabetes, obesity and cancer.

Carrots

Carrots contain carotenoids, flavonoids and polyacetylenes, antioxidants that have been found to help with strengthening eyesight, and lowering cholesterol levels. Carrots have also been shown to have hepatoprotective ("hepato" meaning related to the liver), cardioprotective, antibacterial, antifungal, anti-inflammatory and analgesic effects.

Cayenne Pepper

The active ingredient in cayenne pepper is the compound capsaicin, which has been used as a treatment for reducing pain; may help to boost the metabolism; and has been found to stimulate thermogenesis, the process by which cells convert energy into heat.

Celery

Celery is rich in flavonoids, carotenoids, vitamins, sodium and potassium. Celery juice after a workout serves as a great electrolyte replacement drink. Celery has diuretic effects beneficial for kidney health and contains anutrient compounds known as coumarins, which have been found to enhance the activity of certain white blood cells.

Chia Seeds

Chia seeds are a rich source of protein and fibre and have a healthy omega-3 and omega-6 fatty acid ratio. Chia seeds are considered a functional food because they provide nutritional benefits and contribute to increased satiety and to the prevention of cardiovascular, inflammatory and nervous system diseases.

Cucumbers

Cucumbers contain erepsin, vitamins B1 and C and many other antioxidants that have been found to help lower the risk of chronic diseases such as cardiovascular disease, cancer and diabetes. Cucumbers are also rich in bioactive phytochemicals that have demonstrated anti-inflammatory properties, and their skin is rich in silica, a mineral that supports healthy connective tissues.

Coconut (Oil)

Coconut oil is rich in medium-chain fatty acids, which have been linked with benefits relating to weight control and metabolism. While it is high in saturated fat, coconut oil has been found to boost HDL or "good" cholesterol levels.

Fennel

Fennel contains high levels of flavonoids, specifically quercetin and isoquercetin, which have been linked to capillary health and a strong immune system. Fennel has also demonstrated anti-inflammatory benefits by acting as a strong antihistamine agent.

Collards

Collards are an important source of vitamins C, K and A (in the form of carotenoids). These antioxidants have been associated with a reduced risk of cardiovascular diseases and cancer.

Ginger

Ginger has been found to have antioxidant, antibiotic and antimicrobial properties, all related to the phytochemical gingerol. This flavourful root has also been found to have anti-nausea and anti-inflammatory properties, and has been associated with improved cardiovascular health, thanks to its cholesterol and blood pressure regulating properties.

Grapefruit and Lemons

Grapefruit and lemons are rich in vitamin C, an antioxidant that supports the immune system. Phytonutrients present in these citrus fruits known as limonoids have been linked with cancer prevention and cholesterol management.

Kale

Kale, part of the *Brassica* genus, is rich in vitamins (especially vitamins A, C and K), phenols, carotenoids, glucosinolates, calcium and fibre. Kale has also been found to support the body's detoxification processes.

Honeydew

Honeydew melons are high in vitamin C and potassium. Vitamin C plays an essential role in maintaining a healthy immune system and preventing cardiovascular disease. Potassium is involved in insulin secretion, reducing high blood pressure and helping to reduce the risk of coronary heart disease.

Maca

Maca, a root native to Peru that is ground into a powder and used as a supplement, is rich in B vitamins, minerals, protein and fibre. Proponents of maca point to its energy- and stamina-enhancing properties and its utility in relieving problems related to hormone imbalance. Patients with thyroid conditions should avoid maca.

Jalapeños

Jalapeño peppers contain phenolic compounds called capsaicinoids. Capsaicinoids have been shown to increase energy expenditure and affect appetite, which may have benefits for weight maintenance. These antioxidant molecules have also been found to have anti-inflammatory effects.

Maple (Syrup)

When something sweet is called for, we, being Canadian, lean toward maple syrup. Darker maple syrup, sometimes labelled Grade B or C, "Medium," "Amber" or "Dark," is extracted later in the season and has a more intense flavour. Maple syrup, like all forms of sugar, should be used sparingly, although it does contain minerals such as magnesium and zinc.

Matcha

A finely ground powder made from special green tea that has been shade grown (which stresses the plant, bringing increased nutritional content) and then dried, with the stems removed, matcha's preparation and consumption are at the centre of the traditional Japanese tea ceremony. Matcha has surged in popularity lately, thanks in part to its high antioxidant content.

Red Peppers

Red peppers are known for their rich antioxidant content and are particularly high in vitamin C. The red colour comes from carotenoid pigments including beta carotene, a phytonutrient that can be turned into vitamin A in the body. Vitamin A contributes to normal growth and development, healthy eyes and skin, and a strong immune system.

Romaine

Romaine lettuce has high levels of folate and vitamin B, which contribute to heart and bone health and help to protect eyesight.

Pineapples

Pineapples contain several phytochemicals like coumaric acid and antioxidants like vitamin C that strengthen the immune system and help to improve overall health. Pineapples also contain bromelain, an enzyme that has been reported to exert a wide range of beneficial effects, including assisting with digestion and reducing inflammation.

Spinach

Spinach is high in vitamins, carotenoids, folic acids and minerals including iron and magnesium. This leafy vegetable also has high protein content, offering long-term satiation. Spinach's antioxidant capabilities have been linked with a reduced risk of cancer and many chronic diseases.

Sprouts

Sprouts are good sources of fibre, protein, vitamins and minerals. Sunflower sprouts, for example, offer vitamins C and E, which can improve heart health, boost immunity and support cellular recovery.

Tomatoes

Tomatoes contain the bioactive compounds lycopene and alpha-tomatine. These compounds have been linked to antibiotic, anti-inflammatory, antioxidant, cardiovascular and immune-stimulating benefits.

Turmeric

Turmeric contains the active polyphenol curcumin, which has anti-inflammatory and antioxidant properties that have been linked to a reduced risk of cancer, Alzheimer's disease, heart disease and arthritis. Turmeric has also been used to achieve better skin health.

Swiss Chard

Swiss chard contains a wide range of vitamins, minerals and phenolic compounds. Specifically, Swiss chard is a great source of vitamins A, C, E and K, as well as iron and dietary fibre.

Zucchini

Zucchini has high water content, which can help with puffy eyes and inflammation. Zucchini is also high in immunity boosting vitamin C, and its potassium and magnesium have been found to help lower blood pressure, which supports heart health.

Breakfasts

Dark Cherry Berry Smoothie Bowl

Makes 1 bowl

Smoothie bowls are thicker, more substantial smoothies that you eat with a spoon and top with all kinds of excitement. Thickened by extra fruit or avocado, they should have enough heft to allow granola, berries and coconut flakes to rest atop them, giving you lots of pattern potential. This tart, deep purple bowl is rich in antioxidants, as well as fibre and healthy fats. If you don't have camu camu berry powder, worry not—it provides an extra hit of vitamin C, but this breakfast is just as complete without it.

1 cup Almond Milk (page 219) or other non-dairy milk

½ cup fresh or frozen pitted dark cherries, plus more for garnish

½ cup fresh or frozen blueberries, plus more for garnish

1 tablespoon hemp seeds, plus more for garnish

¼ avocado, pitted

2 Medjool dates, pitted

1 teaspoon camu camu berry powder (found at health food stores or online)

½ teaspoon ground cinnamon

1 teaspoon pure vanilla extract

5 ice cubes

Unsweetened coconut flakes and pomegranate seeds, for serving

Combine the Almond Milk, cherries, blueberries, hemp seeds, avocado, dates, camu camu berry powder, cinnamon and vanilla in a blender.

Blend for 30 seconds, or until well combined. If your blender has more than one speed, start low and slowly build up to medium or high. Taste and adjust if necessary, then add the ice cubes and blend on high until smooth.

Pour into a bowl and top with stripes of your favourite toppings. Serve immediately.

Peach Crisp Smoothie Bowl

Makes 1 bowl

The end of summer is always a bittersweet time, particularly in a northern climate like ours, but we Ontarians find solace in the local produce that becomes available for a brief window at that time of year. While we're certainly proud of our tomatoes, corn and berries, the late August farmstand prom queen is undoubtedly the Ontario peach. They don't stick around for very long, so if you're lucky enough to find them, we recommend slicing up a whole bunch and freezing them. That way you can enjoy this delicate smoothie bowl year-round.

1 cup Almond Milk (page 219) or other non-dairy milk

2 peaches, pitted and sliced

1 frozen banana, roughly chopped

1 teaspoon pure vanilla extract

1 tablespoon pure maple syrup

1 teaspoon coconut oil

½ teaspoon ground cinnamon

6 ice cubes

Granola and extra peach slices, for serving

Combine the Almond Milk, peaches, banana, vanilla, maple syrup, coconut oil and cinnamon in a blender and blend for 30 seconds, or until well combined. If your blender has more than one speed, start low and slowly build up to medium or high. Add the ice cubes and blend on high for another minute or so, until desired consistency is reached.

Pour into your favourite bowl and top with a sprinkle of granola and a few slices of peaches. Serve immediately.

PRO TIP

For a heartier smoothie bowl with more protein and lasting power, add 1 to 2 tablespoons natural almond butter.

Overnight Oats

Makes about 3 servings

Oats that have been soaked overnight have been a staple of healthy breakfasts at least since the turn of the 20th century, when Swiss doctor Maximilian Bircher-Benner started offering his patients a breakfast of soaked oats topped with grated apple as a way of shoehorning more raw fruit into their diets. Softening oats overnight makes them more digestible and increases the bioavailability of their nutrients. It also saves time, rewarding us for our night-before organization with a few precious extra minutes of morning sleep.

1⅓ cups gluten-free rolled oats

2 tablespoons chia seeds

1½ cups Smoothie Milk (page 227) or other unsweetened non-dairy milk

3 to 4 Medjool dates, pitted

1 teaspoon coconut oil

Pinch of ground cinnamon

½ vanilla bean, split lengthwise, seeds scraped out and reserved, or ½ teaspoon pure vanilla extract

Blueberries and chopped nuts or seeds, for serving

PRO TIP

Pure, uncontaminated oats are safe for most people with gluten intolerance. However, oats are often processed in facilities that also process wheat products. If you are allergic to gluten, look for oats labelled "gluten free."

Combine the rolled oats, chia seeds, Smoothie Milk, dates, coconut oil, cinnamon and vanilla seeds or extract in a blender. Blend for about 40 seconds, gradually increasing the speed from low to high, until the mixture is well combined but still viscous and coarse. Pour the mixture into a sealable jar and refrigerate overnight for a quick, hearty, raw breakfast.

This oatmeal tastes great topped with blueberries, sliced bananas, pumpkin seeds, chopped nuts, raisins or even a berry compote, and sprinkled with cinnamon and/or cardamom. Store in a sealed container in the refrigerator for up to 2 days.

VARIATION

MAX IT / For a delicious alternative, reduce or eliminate the dates and add one fresh or frozen ripe banana. Or, to make Maximilian proud, top with a crisp apple that you've sliced thinly (like matchsticks) and mix thoroughly.

Quinoa Banana Pancakes

Makes 6 to 8 pancakes

Waking up to the smell of pancakes sizzling in a hot pan on a weekend morning is one of the best things that can happen to a person. This recipe is lightly sweetened by banana and made fluffy by leftover quinoa. If you don't have any cooked quinoa on hand, you can sub in cooked oatmeal, or just leave it out. We extend our deepest thanks to Angela Liddon, author of *The Oh She Glows Cookbook*, for the cornstarch trick that allows these pancakes to stay together without eggs.

½ cup brown rice flour

½ cup white rice flour

1 tablespoon cornstarch

1 teaspoon baking powder

¾ cup Smoothie Milk (page 227) or other unsweetened non-dairy milk

1 teaspoon pure vanilla extract

1 medium ripe banana, mashed

½ cup cooked white quinoa

2 tablespoons coconut oil

Coconut or vegetable oil for frying

Cashew "Yogurt" (page 39), pure maple syrup and berries, for serving

Preheat the oven to 300°F.

In a medium bowl, mix the brown rice flour, white rice flour, cornstarch and baking powder with a wooden spoon. Pour the Smoothie Milk and vanilla into the mixture and stir until no lumps remain. Be careful not to overmix, or your pancakes will become gummy. Fold in the mashed banana and quinoa.

Preheat a cast-iron skillet or wide frying pan over medium heat. Melt the coconut oil and add it to the batter to help your pancakes achieve that miraculous golden crispiness.

You can either add a bit more coconut oil to your pan for frying (it will lend a slight coconut taste unless you use a dearomatized version) or wipe the remaining coconut oil off of your pan with a paper towel and heat up 1 tablespoon of a neutral-tasting vegetable oil with a high smoke point. Make sure it gets nice and hot. When it's ready, you should see a sheen on the pan and the oil should sizzle like mad if the tiniest drop of water falls onto it (test gently).

Drop about a tablespoon of batter into the pan. Consider this a test pancake. If it doesn't sizzle, your pan isn't hot enough. It's important to let a lot of bubbles form on the surface of the pancake (especially right in the middle) before you attempt to flip. Once the bubbles are out of control and a spatula peek reveals that your test pancake is golden brown on the bottom, flip it and continue to cook for 1 to 2 minutes, until cooked through.

Eat this one while you make the others the same way, two or three at a time. Keep pancakes warm in a baking dish in the oven until the whole batch is ready. Serve with Cashew "Yogurt," maple syrup and berries.

Cashew "Yogurt"

Makes about ¾ cup

Cashews are very often used as a base for dairy alternatives because of their mild, creamy taste. The problem with this is that a person might be justified in complaining, after one cashew garnish too many, that everything is beginning to taste the same. If you can feel yourself turning into a handful of cashews, try making this with Brazil nuts. To make this "yogurt" probiotic, add rejuvelac—a fermented liquid that is extremely digestible and good for your gut. Rejuvelac is the result of soaking and sprouting grains (gluten-free versions are available), is rich in vitamins B, K and E and contains protein and beneficial enzymes. Look for it in the refrigerated section of a health food store.

¾ cup raw cashews, soaked for 2 hours (see page 216)

½ cup filtered water

1 Medjool date, pitted

1 vanilla bean, split lengthwise, seeds scraped out and reserved, or 1 teaspoon pure vanilla extract

1 tablespoon shredded, unsweetened coconut

4 teaspoons freshly squeezed lemon juice

Pinch of sea salt

2 teaspoons ground flax seeds (optional; see pro tip)

½ teaspoon rejuvelac liquid (optional)

Honey and fresh figs, for serving

Combine the cashews, water, date, vanilla seeds or extract, coconut, lemon juice, salt, flax seeds and rejuvelac liquid (if using) in a blender and blend until smooth. Adjust flavour if desired. Serve on Quinoa Banana Pancakes (page 36) with a drizzle of pure maple syrup, or drizzle with honey and top with fresh figs.

PRO TIP

Flax seeds bring omega-3 fatty acids, fibre and thickness. You can purchase it ground, or grind your own in a very clean coffee grinder.

Warming Winter Oatmeal with Roasted Chestnut Purée

Makes 2 servings

In France, *crème de marron* or chestnut cream is ubiquitous and often stirred into a dish of *fromage blanc* (which is similar to yogurt) for breakfast or dessert. We use it here to elevate one of our simplest morning pleasures: a bowl of oats. Select chestnuts that are glossy, unwrinkled and heavy in your palm, with no space between the shell and the meat of the nut inside. Dingy shells and pinholes are bad signs; avoid these chestnuts.

CHESTNUT PURÉE

10 whole chestnuts

¼ cup pure maple syrup

1 vanilla bean, split lengthwise, seeds scraped out and reserved, or 1 teaspoon pure vanilla extract

OATMEAL

2 cups filtered water or non-dairy milk

Pinch of sea salt

1 cup gluten-free rolled oats

Pinch of ground cinnamon

Almond Milk (page 219) or Cashew "Yogurt" (page 39), for serving

Preheat the oven to 400°F.

To make the chestnut purée, wipe the chestnuts clean with a damp cloth and place them flat side down on a cutting board. Using a small, sharp knife, make an X-shaped incision in each chestnut. Cut all the way through the shell until the meat of the chestnut is visible, but be careful not to cut yourself. This step allows steam to escape while the chestnuts are roasting, so they don't explode.

In a rimmed baking pan, roast the chestnuts for 20 to 30 minutes, until the shells have broken open and the chestnuts inside are golden brown. Remove the pan from the oven, cover it with a tea towel, and allow the hot chestnuts to rest for a few minutes in the pan under the towel to let some of the steam escape and help soften them for peeling.

Peel them while they are still warm, removing the hard outer shell and the papery layer underneath. You may want to handle them using gloves or a clean tea towel. Discard any suspicious-looking chestnuts.

Add the peeled chestnuts, maple syrup and vanilla seeds or extract to a food processor or blender and blend to combine. Adjust sweetness and vanilla to taste. The chestnut purée can be made ahead of time and stored in a jar in the fridge for a few days, or you can start making the oatmeal while the chestnuts are roasting.

When you are ready to make the oatmeal, in a medium pot, bring the water or milk and salt to a boil. Add the rolled oats, reduce heat and cook uncovered, stirring occasionally, for about 10 to 20 minutes or until the porridge reaches your desired consistency. Remove from heat, cover and let stand for a few minutes. Swirl in the chestnut purée, top with the cinnamon and Almond Milk or Cashew "Yogurt," and serve immediately.

Vanilla Bean Chia Pudding

Makes 1 to 2 servings

Chia seeds are a complete protein and a source of omega-3s; combined with nut or seed milk and your choice of toppings, we're pretty sure they'll transform your mornings. This recipe is one of our go-to weekday breakfasts: it takes five minutes to whip up before bed, is extremely transportable, and keeps you full for hours.

1 cup Almond Milk (page 219) or other non-dairy milk

3 tablespoons chia seeds

2 tablespoons ground flax seeds

½ vanilla bean, split lengthwise, seeds scraped out and reserved, or ½ teaspoon pure vanilla extract

½ teaspoon maple syrup (optional, if your non-dairy milk is unsweetened)

Pinch of ground cinnamon

Chopped fruit, nuts and seeds, for serving

In a bowl or jar, whisk together the Almond Milk, chia seeds, ground flax seeds, vanilla seeds or extract, maple syrup (if using) and cinnamon. Continue to whisk until the seeds are suspended in the liquid and the mixture has begun to thicken, about 2 minutes. Refrigerate overnight in a sealed container. Serve topped with fresh berries, shaved coconut, sliced bananas, hemp or pumpkin seeds, crumbled walnuts, a scoop of natural almond butter or anything you like. Can be stored in an airtight container in the fridge for up to 2 days.

VARIATION

MATCHA OR CACAO / Omit the cinnamon and whisk in a ½ teaspoon of matcha powder or 1 teaspoon of raw cacao powder instead for an even more energizing breakfast.

Spiced Grain-Free Granola with Brazil Nut Fibre

Makes about 3 cups

So you made some Brazil Nut Milk (page 224) or another nut milk in this book. Now what to do with all the delicious crumbly nut or seed fibre that's left behind in the nut milk bag or cheesecloth? Here is one way to put it to delicious and nutritious use: this tangy, oat-free take on granola provides you with antioxidants, fibre and a full morning's worth of energy.

DATE PASTE

1 cup Medjool dates, pitted

½ cup filtered water

½ tablespoon ground cinnamon

GRANOLA

2½ cups leftover fibre from Brazil Nut Milk (page 224) or any nut or seed milk fibre

2 tablespoons orange zest

3 tablespoons freshly squeezed orange juice

2 tablespoons grated fresh ginger

1 tablespoon ground cinnamon

1 tablespoon pure vanilla extract

3 tablespoons pure maple syrup

½ cup raw sunflower seeds

½ teaspoon sea salt

3 tablespoons date paste (recipe above)

¼ cup coconut oil, melted

1 cup unsweetened coconut flakes (optional)

1 cup dried fruit (optional)

¼ cup hemp seeds, whole flax seeds or chia seeds (optional)

Preheat the oven to 250°F. Line two baking sheets with parchment paper and set aside.

To make the date paste, place the dates, water and cinnamon in a food processor or blender and blend until smooth and creamy. Set aside.

To make the granola, in a large bowl, combine the Brazil nut fibre, orange zest, orange juice, ginger, cinnamon, vanilla, maple syrup, sunflower seeds and salt. Stir in 3 tablespoons of the date paste and then add the coconut oil and combine well.

Spread the mixture evenly onto the lined baking sheets and bake for 1½ to 2 hours, or until golden, stirring every 15 minutes or so for even browning. Allow the granola to cool, then add coconut flakes, dried fruit and additional seeds (if using). Store in a sealed container for 1 to 2 weeks.

Ancient Grain, Seed and Nut Loaf

Makes 1 loaf or about 10 slices

This is a dark, dense bread that, thanks to the nuts and seeds, holds its heat beautifully when toasted. Try it as a base for homemade Chocolate Hazelnut Spread (page 49, because chocolate for breakfast is always a good idea), Avocado Toast with Harissa and Sprouts (page 50), Warm Beet Hummus (page 99), or all by its lonesome. We are grateful to Sarah Britton, author of *My New Roots*, for planting the seed for this recipe with her Life-Changing Loaf of Bread. It has indeed changed our lives.

½ cup raw sunflower seeds

¾ cup raw pumpkin seeds

1 cup raw slivered almonds

⅛ cup buckwheat groats

⅛ cup millet seeds

⅓ cup amaranth seeds

1½ cups gluten-free rolled oats

¾ cups gluten-free steel-cut oats

⅓ cup whole flax seeds

⅓ cup psyllium seed husks

⅓ cup chia seeds

2 teaspoons sea salt

2 tablespoons pure maple syrup

¼ cup virgin olive oil

2¾ cups filtered water

PRO TIP

The ingredients can be found in the bulk food section of your health food store. If you cannot find either millet seeds or amaranth seeds, just use one and adjust the quantity accordingly. Same goes for rolled oats and steel-cut oats.

Preheat the oven to 325°F. Line a baking sheet with parchment paper.

Combine and evenly spread the sunflower seeds, pumpkin seeds, almonds, buckwheat groats, millet seeds and amaranth seeds on the prepared baking sheet. Toast for 10 to 12 minutes, or until golden.

In a large bowl, combine the rolled oats, steel-cut oats, flax seeds, psyllium seed husks, chia seeds and salt.

When the toasting seed mixture is golden, remove from the oven and add to the bowl of dry ingredients; stir until combined. Add the maple syrup, olive oil and water to the bowl and mix well. We use our hands for this (wet them first). The mixture should feel quite soggy; the seeds will absorb more water as they rest.

Line the bottom and sides of an 8- × 4-inch or 9- × 5-inch loaf pan with parchment paper. Pour the dough into the pan and shape the top into a smooth dome with wet fingers. Cover the dough with a clean tea towel or napkin and let it sit at room temperature overnight or for up to 24 hours.

When you're ready to bake, preheat the oven to 400°F.

Uncover the dough and place the loaf pan on a rack in the centre of the oven. Bake for an hour and 15 minutes, or until the crust is dark brown and sounds hollow when you knock on it. (It may take an hour and a half, depending on your oven.) Remove loaf from the oven and let cool completely, at least 2 hours.

Slice and serve toasted. Store in a sealed container in the fridge for 1 to 2 weeks.

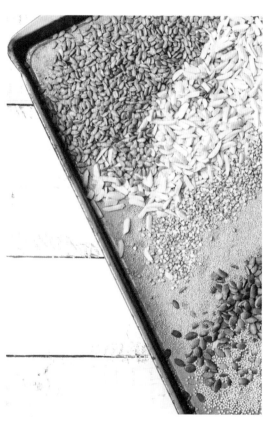

Chocolate Hazelnut Spread

Makes ½ cup

This is a homemade, less sweet version of one of our favourite childhood treats. Spread it on the Ancient Grain, Seed and Nut Loaf (page 46) and top with a sprinkle of cinnamon, hemp seeds, sliced bananas or smashed raspberries.

1 cup raw hazelnuts

¾ cup filtered water

4 Medjool dates, pitted

Pinch of sea salt

1 tablespoon coconut oil

2 tablespoons raw cacao
or cocoa powder

½ vanilla bean, split lengthwise,
seeds scraped out and reserved,
or ½ teaspoon pure vanilla extract

Preheat the oven to 350°F. Line a baking sheet with parchment paper.

Spread the hazelnuts on the baking sheet and roast for 7 to 10 minutes, until fragrant and lightly darkened. Be careful not to burn them. Remove the hazelnuts from the oven and let them cool. Once cooled, remove the hazelnut skins with your fingers.

Place the skinned, roasted hazelnuts, water, dates, salt, coconut oil, cacao powder and vanilla seeds or extract in a blender. Blend on medium and then high for about 30 seconds. Taste. You may need to add an additional teaspoon or two of water or coconut oil and blend again on high to achieve maximum smoothness. A chunky, more rustic version is great, too.

Enjoy on the toast of your choice or straight from the spoon. Store in an airtight container in the fridge for up to 3 days.

Avocado Toast with Harissa and Sprouts

Makes about 1 cup harissa and 2 slices of avocado toast

Nothing elevates avocado toast quite like a spicy layer of harissa. A hot chili paste most closely linked to Tunisia, Algeria and Libya, harissa varies widely by region; there may be as many unique varieties as there are families who make it. Ours is made with guajillo chili, which is actually a Mexican pepper and is useful here because it is full of flavour but not overwhelmingly spicy. It lasts well in the fridge and is an extraordinarily versatile condiment; try it with the Lentils and Brown Rice with Rainbow Chard, Roasted Carrots and Tahini (page 79) or the Moroccan Sweet Potato Hash (page 53). If you're pressed for time, use a store-bought harissa: you can find it in tubes or jars in most well-stocked grocery stores.

HARISSA

18 dried guajillo peppers

1 cup virgin olive oil

1 head garlic, peeled and coarsely chopped

1½ teaspoons sea salt

1 tablespoon coarsely chopped preserved lemon

4 sundried tomatoes, coarsely chopped

3 teaspoons ancho chili powder

2 tablespoons dried cumin

2 teaspoons ground cayenne pepper

AVOCADO TOAST

2 slices of your favourite bread (we use the Ancient Grain, Seed and Nut Loaf on page 46)

1 tablespoon virgin olive oil, divided

2 to 4 teaspoons harissa (recipe above)

1 avocado, pitted and sliced

1 to 2 teaspoons freshly squeezed lemon juice

Pinch of sea salt

½ cup sprouts of your choice

For the harissa, using kitchen scissors, cut off the stems of the dried guajillo peppers and then snip the peppers into thin ribbons.

In a small pot on low heat, add the guajillo peppers, olive oil, garlic and salt. Lightly brown the garlic, about 6 to 8 minutes, and remove from heat. In a food processor, combine all the ingredients from the pot with the preserved lemon, sundried tomatoes, ancho chili powder, cumin and cayenne. Process all ingredients on low speed, then medium and then high for 30 seconds to a minute, or until the harissa is smooth. The harissa will turn out very dark red and medium-hot. Store it in a sealed jar in the fridge. It will last for several weeks.

To prepare the avocado toast, toast your bread to your preferred level of crispiness, either in a toaster, under the broiler or in a cast-iron pan with a bit of olive oil. Smear about 1 tablespoon harissa onto the toast.

Slice the avocado in ¼-inch-thick slices and cover the toast with avocado slices. Each slice of bread will fit about half an avocado, depending on the size of your bread.

Sprinkle the lemon juice on the top of the avocado, plus a tiny pinch of salt and a small drizzle of olive oil. Finally, cover with the sprouts, about 1 heaping tablespoon per slice. Serve immediately.

Moroccan Sweet Potato Hash

Makes 2 servings

Hana brought this for me to try one day when we were working late into the night at our production facility. I couldn't find a spoon, nor could I wait until I got home (it smelled too good), so we sat on a bench outside and I ate it using two bottle caps as chopsticks (Hana's invention), and then with my fingers. I can say with authority that this recipe is absolutely worth dying your fingertips orange for.

1 large sweet potato, peeled and cubed

2½ tablespoons virgin olive oil, divided

Pinch of sea salt and freshly ground black pepper

2 shallots, finely chopped

1 clove garlic, minced

4 cups white or brown mushrooms, stems removed, rubbed clean, chopped into quarters

5 large kale leaves, veins removed and thinly sliced

½ teaspoon ground cumin

½ teaspoon ground turmeric

Pinch of hot paprika

Pinch of ground ginger or ½ teaspoon finely chopped fresh ginger

Pinch of ground cinnamon

Pinch of ground cayenne pepper

Preheat the oven to 375°F. Line a baking sheet with parchment paper and set aside.

In a medium bowl, toss the sweet potato with ½ tablespoon olive oil and a pinch of salt and pepper. Spread onto the prepared baking sheet and bake for 25 minutes or until lightly crisped.

While the sweet potatoes are baking, sauté the shallots in a large pan over medium heat in 1 tablespoon olive oil for 30 seconds, or until fragrant. Add the garlic and continue cooking until the shallots are soft and slightly brown. Add the mushrooms and continue cooking over medium heat for 8 to 10 minutes, until the mushrooms have softened. Add the kale and allow it to wilt slightly.

When the cooked sweet potatoes are done, add them to the sauté pan and mix everything together well. Add the spices and the remaining 1 tablespoon of olive oil. Mix to combine. When the kale is slightly crisped and wilted, remove from heat. Serve and enjoy!

PRO TIP

Instead of using ground turmeric and ginger, use 3 teaspoons turmeric juice and 3 teaspoons ginger juice for an extra kick!

For some extra protein, serve with grilled tofu (see page 70) or a poached egg (if such a thing appeals to you).

Lunches and Dinners

Pea Shoot and Asparagus Salad with Toasted Hazelnuts

Serves 4 as a side or 2 as a main

In the early days of Greenhouse, I would often wander over to my dad's house, which is not far from our original shop, for a restorative weeknight supper. My dad delights in experimenting and can always whip up something breathtaking from whatever happens to be in his fridge. He regularly entertains while cooking, and it's common to be so engrossed in what he's saying that you don't notice him chopping, blanching, sautéing or searing; when a perfectly timed, perfectly proportioned plate appears in front of you, it's like a magic trick. This spring salad is one of his many inventions.

SALAD

1 bunch asparagus (around 12 spears), trimmed

1 teaspoon coarse sea salt, divided

½ cup shelled fresh green peas (frozen work too, but fresh is ideal in spring or summer)

2 cups loosely packed pea shoots

½ cup whole hazelnuts

Freshly ground black pepper

Edible flowers, for serving (optional)

VINAIGRETTE

⅓ cup virgin olive oil

2 tablespoons plus 2 teaspoons white wine vinegar

Pinch of cane sugar (optional; helps to make flavours pop)

VARIATION

PECORINO / The original version of this salad also includes sharp pecorino, sliced into ¼-inch cubes roughly equal in size and quantity to the hazelnuts. The saltiness is a perfect complement to the sweet peas or a sliced avocado is another good accompaniment. Toss either in last after the salad is dressed.

Preheat the oven to 350°F.

To make the salad, start by blanching the asparagus. Prepare an ice bath by filling a bowl or casserole dish with 2 inches of very cold water and a handful of ice cubes.

Fill a wide, shallow pan with enough water to cover the asparagus. Bring the water to a vigorous boil and throw your asparagus in. Blanch it until it is deep green and tender, but still crunchy—approximately 1 minute for skinny spring asparagus or up to 2 minutes for fat summer asparagus. Be careful not to leave it in too long; soggy, limp asparagus is no one's idea of a good time.

Remove the asparagus from the boiling water with tongs and drop it in the ice bath. Submerge the spears until you are satisfied that they are thoroughly chilled, then lay them on a double layer of paper towel. Sprinkle a good amount of salt over them, wrap them up in the paper towel, and place them in the fridge.

Repeat the method above to blanch the peas, (This can also be done simultaneously if you have two pans and are cool under pressure).

Toast the hazelnuts on a baking sheet in the oven or in a skillet over medium heat for 5 minutes, or until fragrant and crunchy. Set a timer so you don't forget about them. Sprinkle some salt on them while they're still hot and let them cool. (You can rub off the skins if you'd like, but it's not necessary.)

To make the vinaigrette, in a small bowl, mix the olive oil, white wine vinegar and sugar (if using). Place the pea shoots in a salad bowl and toss with the vinaigrette, ensuring they are well coated. Slice your cold, crunchy asparagus into ½-inch pieces and mix them into the salad along with the peas and cooled hazelnuts. Crack black pepper on top to taste, and serve.

Kale Salad with Roasted Beets and Avocado

Serves 4 as a side or 2 as a main

This salad finds sweetness from roasted beets, saltiness from black olives (we use wrinkly Moroccans), richness from toasted pine nuts and avocado, freshness from parsley and excitement from raw garlic—meaning that it has enough going for it to stand up as a meal, and to hold your attention to the bottom of the bowl. "Massaging" vinaigrette into torn pieces of kale is a great way to soften this notoriously brawny leaf and make it more palatable in its raw form.

VINAIGRETTE
(makes twice what you need for the salad; save the other half in a jar in the fridge)

⅓ cup virgin olive oil

¼ cup freshly squeezed lemon juice

2 tablespoons Dijon mustard (pale yellow, not grainy)

1 clove garlic, minced

Plenty of ground pepper (4 to 5 grinds)

SALAD

1 bunch green or red kale (about 4 cups)

3 small or 2 medium beets

2 tablespoons virgin olive oil

½ teaspoon sea salt

¼ cup pine nuts

2 tablespoons finely torn or chopped parsley

½ cup black olives, pitted and sliced in half

½ ripe avocado, pitted and sliced

Preheat the oven to 400°F. Line a baking sheet with parchment paper and set aside.

To make the vinaigrette, whisk together the olive oil, lemon juice, mustard, minced garlic and pepper.

To make the salad, strip the kale leaves from their stems by holding them upside down and pulling the leaves downward. Tear them into bite-sized pieces. Place kale in a large salad bowl and set aside.

Slice off the ends of your beets. (Save the greens; they're yummy steamed or sautéed in a bit of olive oil with salt.) Peel the beets and chop them into somewhat uniform ½-inch pieces. Toss the beet pieces in the olive oil and salt. Spread in a single layer on the prepared baking sheet. Roast for 20 to 22 minutes, or until tender with a bit of crispiness (but be careful not to dry them out). About 15 minutes in, shuffle the beets around with a wooden spoon or spatula to help them roast evenly. Remove from the oven and let cool.

In a small skillet on the stove, toast the pine nuts for 5 to 6 minutes, shaking the pan to toast evenly. Remove from skillet and let cool.

Pour half of the vinaigrette over the kale, massaging it into the leaves with your hands. For optimal kale texture and vinaigrette absorption, you really have to rub it in. Add the chopped parsley and pitted and sliced olives to the kale. When you're ready to serve, scatter the beets and pine nuts onto the salad and top with slices of avocado.

PRO TIP

This salad does well in a packed lunch—just add the pine nuts and avocado last and squeeze some lemon on the avocado to keep it from browning. Consider serving topped with some grilled slices of halloumi, shaved ricotta salata or, for a *fattoush* touch, toasted or fried triangles of leftover pita.

Broccoli Soup with Sweet Potato Croutons

Makes 4 to 6 bowls

Earthy, grounding and filling, this soup is most comforting when served hot in a steaming mug or bowl. Sweet potato croutons provide a textural contrast as well as fibre and antioxidants. Cashew cream adds a cooling touch of luxury and looks impressive when you swirl it through with a drizzle of balsamic. We like to serve this with Flax Crackers with Black Olives (page 108) or a slice of Ancient Grain, Seed and Nut Loaf (page 46) with Roasted Eggplant Dip (page 100). If you have a homemade vegetable broth, replace the water and salt in this soup with broth.

CASHEW CREAM

⅔ cup raw cashews, soaked (see page 216)

½ cup filtered water

SOUP

2 tablespoons virgin olive oil

2 leeks (see pro tip) or 1 white onion, coarsely chopped

5¼ cups filtered water or vegetable broth, divided

2 cloves garlic, minced

1 medium carrot, coarsely chopped

2 heads broccoli, chopped into florets and stems peeled and chopped into ¼-inch-thick coins (about 8 cups)

2 bay leaves

2 teaspoons freshly squeezed lemon juice

Up to 1 tablespoon sea salt, divided

Several grinds of freshly ground black pepper, to taste

Dash of aged balsamic vinegar or balsamic reduction, for garnish

Pinch of sweet paprika, for garnish

SWEET POTATO CROUTONS

2 large sweet potatoes, scrubbed, skin on, chopped into ½-inch cubes

2 tablespoons virgin olive oil

½ teaspoon sea salt

1 to 2 teaspoons sweet paprika

1 teaspoon dried oregano

Drain and rinse the soaked cashews and add them to a blender with ½ cup water. Blend on high until a smooth, creamy consistency is reached. Set aside.

Preheat the oven to 425°F. Line a baking sheet with parchment paper and set aside.

To make the soup, warm the olive oil in a large soup pot over medium heat. Add the leeks or onions and a pinch of salt and sauté for 2 to 3 minutes, or until they start to soften, stirring often. Add ¼ cup water or broth if needed to prevent the leeks from sticking to the bottom of the pan. Add the garlic and sauté until golden and fragrant. Then add the carrots and sauté until they start to soften, about 10 minutes. Add up to ½ cup more water or broth as needed to avoid burning the garlic, leeks or carrots.

Add the chopped broccoli florets and stems to the pot with another ½ cup water or broth and cover the pot to allow the broccoli to steam; it will take on a deeper green as it softens. Add the remaining 4 cups water or broth and the bay leaves. Bring to a boil, then reduce heat to a simmer. If you are using water, stir in the salt and several grinds of black pepper to taste; use less salt or no salt if you are using broth. Let it simmer for 15 to 20 minutes with the lid on.

Meanwhile, make the sweet potato croutons. Place the sweet potato cubes in a large mixing bowl and add the olive oil, salt, paprika and oregano. Mix to distribute seasoning evenly. Spread the seasoned cubes on the baking sheet, leaving space between the croutons. This is important to get them crispy (or else they will steam). Roast for 20 to 30 minutes. Check on them after 10 minutes, moving them around with a wooden spoon or spatula. You may need to turn the oven down to 400°F if it gets too hot. When done, remove croutons from the oven.

Once your soup has simmered for 15 to 20 minutes, remove the bay leaves. Add the lemon juice and black pepper, taste

(RECIPE CONTINUES)

and adjust salt if needed. Working in batches, add the hot soup to a blender or food processor that can handle heat (or use an immersion blender), and blend on high until smooth and velvety.

Ladle your soup into bowls and top each with a tablespoon of cashew cream and a drizzle of balsamic vinegar or balsamic reduction, swirling them through with a spoon. Garnish with a handful of sweet potato croutons and a pinch of paprika.

The soup can be made in advance and kept for 2 to 3 days in the fridge. The croutons should be made just before eating or they will lose their crunch.

PRO TIP

To wash leeks, slice off the bottom ½ inch and top 3 to 6 inches and remove the two outer skins. Create one long vertical incision on either side of the leek, slicing halfway through the layers to the core. Hold the leek under cold running water while you open the layers and let the water wash the dirt into the sink.

Tuscan White Bean Soup with Dinosaur Kale

Makes 4 to 6 bowls

This is a hearty, restorative soup for a cold night. White beans are an excellent source of fibre and protein. We use dinosaur kale, which is also sometimes known as lacinato or black kale, because we like how its coarse texture stands up to the soup; if you can't find dinosaur kale, you can replace it with another kind of kale or with another leafy green, such as collards or chard. Serve with a green salad and a thick slice of bread rubbed with garlic and drizzled with olive oil.

5 tablespoons virgin olive oil, divided

2 medium onions, coarsely chopped

2 medium carrots, chopped into thin rounds

4 stalks celery, chopped

3 cloves garlic, minced

2 bay leaves

5 cups filtered water or vegetable broth

4 cups cooked white beans (cannellini, great northern or navy beans)

1 bunch dinosaur kale, chopped into ribbons (about 3 cups)

Up to 4¼ teaspoons sea salt, divided

Up to 2 teaspoons freshly ground black pepper, divided

1 cup cherry tomatoes, sliced in half

2 teaspoons aged balsamic vinegar, divided

2 sprigs flat-leaf or curly parsley, for garnish

Preheat the oven to 400°F. Line a baking sheet with parchment paper and set aside.

In a large pot, warm 2 tablespoons olive oil over medium heat. Sauté the onions for about 7 minutes, until fragrant and beginning to soften, then add the carrots and sauté for 5 minutes. Add the celery, garlic and 2 more tablespoons of olive oil and sauté for 5 to 7 minutes, until the garlic is golden and fragrant.

Add the bay leaves and water or broth to the pot, along with the white beans and kale. If you are using water, stir in the salt and several grinds of black pepper to taste; use less or no salt if you are using broth. Reduce the heat to low, cover and let simmer for about 15 minutes, stirring occasionally.

Meanwhile, in a small bowl, coat the cherry tomatoes in the remaining 1 tablespoon olive oil, 1 teaspoon balsamic vinegar and a pinch of salt. Spread the tomatoes on the prepared baking sheet and roast for 20 minutes, checking on them after 10 minutes and shifting them around with a wooden spoon or spatula. The tomatoes are ready once they are shrivelled and dark red.

When you are ready to serve your soup, remove the bay leaves from the pot and stir in the roasted tomatoes, along with the remaining 1 teaspoon of balsamic vinegar and an extra grind or two of fresh black pepper. Garnish with a few leaves of parsley and serve. This soup lasts for several days in the fridge; sometimes it tastes even better on the second and third days.

Socca with Walnut Pesto and Arugula

Serves 4 to 6 as a starter or 2 to 4 as a main

Socca, also known as *farinata*, is a kind of flatbread made from chickpea flour that's popular across Italy and in the south of France. It is sometimes baked in a pizza oven, sometimes in a cast-iron pan and sometimes on a rimmed baking sheet or dish—use what's available to you. It pairs perfectly with a smear of pesto, a pile of arugula, some cherry tomatoes and perhaps a few slices of buffalo mozzarella.

SOCCA

1 cup chickpea flour

1 teaspoon sea salt

Pinch of freshly ground black pepper

1¼ cups filtered water

Virgin olive oil for greasing pan and for garnish (about 2 tablespoons)

3 cups arugula

½ cup cherry tomatoes, sliced in half (optional)

Juice of ½ lemon

WALNUT PESTO

4 cups loosely packed basil leaves

15 walnuts, crushed (½ cup when whole or in large pieces)

4 tablespoons virgin olive oil

3 tablespoons nutritional yeast

2 cloves garlic, peeled

1 tablespoon freshly squeezed lemon juice

¼ teaspoon sea salt

Pinch of freshly ground black pepper

Begin by making the batter for the socca; it needs time to sit. In a large bowl, combine the flour with the salt and black pepper. Vigorously whisk in the water to avoid clumping. It should have the consistency of cream. Cover with a tea towel and let sit at room temperature for a minimum of an hour, or overnight.

Once the batter has rested, preheat the oven to 425°F.

Grease a rimmed 11- × 17-inch baking sheet with olive oil. Whisk the batter and pour it into the baking sheet (it should be about ⅛ to ¼ inch thick). Bake for 20 minutes, or until the batter has set. Broil for another 5 minutes, until the top is golden and crisp. Check often to avoid burning.

While the socca is baking, prepare the pesto. Wash the basil and remove the stems. In a food processor, combine the basil leaves, walnuts, olive oil, nutritional yeast, garlic, lemon juice, salt and pepper. Blend on low, then increase speed to medium for about 40 seconds.

Once the socca is done, remove it from the oven and let it cool. Slice it into large triangles or squares and carefully remove each piece using a spatula. To serve, smear pesto onto each slice. Add a small handful of arugula on top of the pesto, a drizzle of olive oil, some sliced cherry tomatoes (if using), a crack of black pepper and a squeeze of lemon.

Quinoa Pilaf "Chicoutimi" with Peas, Napa Cabbage and Mint

Makes 4 to 6 servings

This is a pilaf that comes by way of the northeast of Quebec, from whence hails Denyse Green, nicknamed "Chicoutimi" by her eldest son, Anthony. This recipe is in fact a second-generation pilaf "Chicoutimi" perfected by Denyse's daughter Deeva, and it is a wonderfully satisfying one-dish meal.

1½ cups red quinoa

3 cups vegetable broth

2 tablespoons virgin olive oil, divided

5 cups button mushrooms, stems removed, rubbed clean, chopped into quarters

2 cloves garlic, minced

Pinch of sea salt, or to taste

½ teaspoon balsamic vinegar

4 cups densely packed chopped napa cabbage or dinosaur kale

½ cup fresh or frozen peas

1½ tablespoons tamari

1 teaspoon apple cider vinegar

1 teaspoon sesame oil

½ teaspoon ground cayenne pepper

1 tablespoon freshly squeezed lemon juice

½ cup loosely packed, finely chopped fresh mint, plus extra leaves, for garnish

Rinse the quinoa in a fine-mesh sieve. In a medium pot, combine the quinoa and broth. Bring to a boil, then reduce heat to low and cook, covered, for 12 to 15 minutes, until the liquid has been absorbed. Turn off the heat and let the quinoa stand for at least 5 minutes. Fluff with a fork and reserve, covered.

In a large pan, heat 1 tablespoon olive oil over medium heat. Add the mushrooms and stir with a wooden spoon or spatula. Add the garlic and a pinch of salt. Sauté for 5 to 7 minutes, until the mushrooms are brown and fragrant. Add the balsamic vinegar, sauté for another minute and set aside.

In another large pan with a lid (or using the same pan, minus the mushrooms), heat the remaining 1 tablespoon olive oil over medium heat. Add the cabbage or kale and cook, covered, for 5 to 7 minutes, stirring occasionally, until soft but not limp.

Cook the peas in a small pot of boiling water for 1 minute, or until they have softened (if fresh) or thawed (if frozen), but still have a bit of crunch. Drain and reserve.

In a large, wide pan, combine the cooked quinoa, tamari, apple cider vinegar, sesame oil and cayenne. Slowly stir in the mushrooms, cabbage or kale and peas. Warm if needed. Add the lemon juice and fresh mint and continue mixing gently. Taste. Add extra cayenne if desired, and garnish with extra mint leaves. Serve hot.

This dish keeps in the fridge for about 3 days and makes for excellent take-away lunches and leftovers.

Spaghetti Squash with Ginger, Chili, Lime and Grilled Tofu

Serves 4 to 6

This dish is inspired by the Filipino staple known as *pancit*. We've substituted spaghetti squash for the traditional mung bean or rice noodles. The result is a light, spicy "noodle" dish anchored with hearty wedges of grilled tofu.

2 medium-large spaghetti squash, sliced lengthwise, seeds removed

1 tablespoon virgin olive oil

One 8-ounce package extra-firm tofu

2 tablespoons plus 2 teaspoons tamari, divided

3 teaspoons Bragg's Liquid Aminos, divided

1 tablespoon coconut oil, divided

Two 1-inch pieces fresh ginger, peeled and sliced into thin slivers

3 cloves garlic, minced

2 medium carrots, peeled and sliced diagonally

2 cups green beans, ends trimmed and sliced diagonally

Juice of 2 limes, divided

½ teaspoon chili flakes, plus more for garnish or to taste

2 tablespoons finely chopped cilantro, plus extra leaves for garnish

Preheat the oven to 400°F. Line a baking sheet with parchment paper and set aside.

Rub the inside of the squash with the olive oil, place it skin side up on the prepared baking sheet and bake for about 45 minutes, until soft inside.

While the squash is baking, prepare the tofu. Rinse the tofu and dry it with paper towel, then slice it into ¼-inch-thick triangles. In a medium bowl, combine 2 tablespoons tamari and 2 teaspoons Bragg's. Add the tofu to this mixture and marinate for up to 2 hours, turning it over occasionally.

To prepare the vegetables, heat ½ tablespoon coconut oil in a large skillet or wok over medium heat. Add the ginger and garlic and sauté for 1 minute. Add the carrots and cook for 2 minutes, stirring often. Add the green beans and cook for another 5 minutes. When the vegetables are al dente, remove from heat and set aside.

To grill the tofu, warm the remaining ½ tablespoon coconut oil on a grill pan on medium-high heat; grill for 60 to 90 seconds, or until golden brown. Flip and repeat on the other side.

Once the squash is cooked, remove it from the oven and allow it to cool. When it is cool enough to handle, use a fork to scrape the squash flesh out lengthwise, moving the fork from one end to the other; the flesh will become spaghetti-like. Place the squash in a strainer and let it drain for 5 to 10 minutes. Discard the water and gently stir the spaghetti squash into the pan of vegetables. Add the juice of ½ a lime, the remaining 2 teaspoons tamari and remaining 1 teaspoon Bragg's (or to taste), the chili flakes and the chopped cilantro.

To serve, arrange the spaghetti squash and vegetables in a large, shallow serving dish or into individual bowls and top with triangles of tofu. Garnish with cilantro leaves, the remaining lime juice and additional chili flakes.

Miso-Glazed Eggplant, Kabocha Squash and Black Rice

Serves 4

Miso-glazed eggplant, known in Japan as *nasu dengaku*, is one of our all-time favourite things to eat. While elongated Japanese eggplants are ideal for this dish, any eggplant will work. If you don't have sake on hand, sub in mirin.

KABOCHA SQUASH

1 large or 2 small kabocha squash, halved, seeds removed, cut into ½-inch slices

1 tablespoon virgin olive oil

Pinch of sea salt

1 teaspoon sweet paprika

BLACK RICE

1 cup short-grain black rice

2 cups filtered water

Pinch of sea salt

1 clove garlic, peeled

1-inch piece fresh ginger, peeled and cut in half

1 tablespoon toasted sesame oil

1 teaspoon tamari

MISO-GLAZED EGGPLANT

2 medium Japanese eggplants, sliced in half lengthwise and scored

1 to 2 tablespoons virgin olive oil (plus more, or water, if needed)

1 tablespoon sake

1 tablespoon mirin

2 tablespoons light miso paste

1 tablespoon pure maple syrup

GARNISH

Chili flakes, sesame seeds and sliced green onions

Preheat the oven to 400°F. Line two baking sheets with parchment paper and set aside.

Coat the squash slices in the olive oil, salt and paprika and spread them out on one of the prepared baking sheets. Roast for about 35 minutes, flipping them over after 15 minutes. The squash is ready once all the flesh is golden, the exterior is a bit crispy and the interior is soft. Remove from the oven and reduce the heat to 350°F.

While the squash is roasting, cook the rice. Rinse the rice under cold water, then add it to a medium pot with the water, salt, garlic and ginger. Bring to a boil, then let simmer over low heat with a tight lid for about 25 to 35 minutes. Once the rice is perfectly al dente, remove from heat. Remove the ginger, mash in the garlic with a fork and cover. Mix in the sesame oil and tamari.

To prepare the eggplants, slice them in half lengthwise, and score the flesh with a sharp knife. Add the olive oil to a large pan over medium heat. Lay the eggplant slices in a single layer in the pan (skin side down) and cover. Cook until browned and very soft, adding more olive oil or a bit of water (1 tablespoon at a time) if needed to keep them moist.

Meanwhile, in a small saucepan over medium heat, combine the sake, mirin and miso, and whisk until smooth. Turn the heat down to low, stir in the maple syrup, and simmer.

Transfer the eggplants to the second prepared baking sheet in a single layer, and spoon a generous amount of miso glaze onto each slice. Bake for 10 to 12 minutes, or until the eggplants are cooked through and the glaze is bubbling.

To serve, arrange the rice, squash and eggplant in bento boxes or on individual plates. Garnish with chili flakes, sesame seeds and green onions.

Summer Ratatouille with Creamy Polenta

Serves 4 to 6

Some ratatouilles are more delicate than this version; ours is a hearty dish that stands up as a meal unto itself. We use leeks instead of onions, but the choice is yours; leeks add a lovely taste, but also tend to sprawl throughout the dish and make themselves seen, whereas onions are more discreet. The creamy polenta acts as the perfect base for this wonderful mess.

RATATOUILLE

3 medium tomatoes, sliced
into ¼-inch rounds

3 red peppers, seeds removed,
sliced into 1-inch wedges

5 tablespoons virgin
olive oil, divided

1 teaspoon sea salt, divided

5 cloves garlic, minced

3 leeks, halved lengthwise, then
sliced into 1-inch-thick pieces (or
2 white onions, coarsely chopped)

3 medium eggplants, sliced into
½-inch-thick rounds, then quartered

2 medium zucchini, sliced into
½-inch-thick rounds, then quartered

2 cups canned, diced tomatoes

2 bay leaves

1 tablespoon herbes de Provence

½ teaspoon freshly
ground black pepper

2 tablespoons freshly
squeezed lemon juice

4 to 5 basil leaves, for garnish

POLENTA

5 cups filtered water,
plus more if needed

1½ teaspoons sea salt

1 cup polenta (cornmeal)

Preheat the oven to 425°F. Line a baking sheet with parchment and set aside.

In a medium bowl, mix the tomatoes and peppers with 1 tablespoon olive oil and a pinch of salt. Add the garlic. Place the tomatoes and red peppers on the baking sheet. Roast for about 25 minutes, moving the vegetables around with a wooden spoon or spatula after 10 minutes, and again after 20, to keep them from burning.

To cook the remaining vegetables, heat 1 tablespoon olive oil in a large pan on medium heat. Add the leeks or onions, eggplants, zucchini and a pinch of salt. Stir, cover and let soften for about 10 minutes, adding ¼ cup water as needed to prevent them from sticking to the pan. Uncover and continue to sauté until quite soft. Stir in the diced tomatoes, bay leaves and herbes de Provence. Add the roasted tomatoes, red peppers and garlic, and simmer on low for another 20 to 30 minutes, stirring occasionally.

While all the vegetables are cooking together, make the polenta. Bring 5 cups water to a boil with 1½ teaspoons salt. Turn the heat down to low to avoid splatter. Very slowly, add the dry polenta to the boiling water, whisking as you go to keep clumps from forming. Cook without a lid for 30 to 45 minutes, whisking every few minutes. The polenta is ready when it acquires a viscous, even consistency, a bit like porridge. If it gets too thick, add ½ cup water and stir. Add 1 tablespoon olive oil before serving.

Finish the ratatouille with the remaining 1 to 2 tablespoons olive oil, remaining ½ teaspoon salt (or more to taste), a few grinds of black pepper and the lemon juice. Serve on a bed of the soft, creamy polenta. Garnish with fresh basil leaves.

Spicy Mushroom Tacos with Crispy Tempeh

Makes 12 tacos

Originally from Indonesia, tempeh is one of our favourite plant proteins. Made from fermented grains or beans, it has a toothsome texture and absorbs flavour very well. Denser than tofu, both in bite and in nutritional assets, it crisps beautifully. If you are looking to reduce your reliance on soy, there are now soy-free varieties of tempeh available. Here we marinate the tempeh in a mix of tamari, Bragg's Liquid Aminos and miso paste. In both the tempeh marinade and the umami sauce, you can use light or dark miso; we prefer light because it's sweeter. We like to serve these tacos with a slice of avocado and a generous smear of umami spicy sauce, which we use as an all-purpose condiment.

UMAMI SPICY SAUCE

2 tablespoons light miso paste

2 tablespoons red curry paste

4 teaspoons tamari

1 teaspoon virgin olive oil

2 teaspoons sesame oil

2 teaspoons hot chili flakes

3 teaspoons freshly squeezed lemon juice

TEMPEH

3 tablespoons tamari (see pro tip)

3 tablespoons Bragg's Liquid Aminos (see pro tip)

1 tablespoon light miso paste

3 tablespoons filtered water

One 8-ounce package tempeh, cut into ½-inch-thick strips

Coconut oil for baking sheet

TACOS

1 teaspoon virgin olive oil

1 bunch green onions, finely chopped (approximately 2 cups)

2 cloves garlic, minced

½ teaspoon finely grated fresh ginger

To make the umami spicy sauce, combine the miso, curry paste, tamari, olive oil, sesame oil, chili flakes, and lemon juice in a small bowl and whisk thoroughly. Set aside.

Preheat the oven to 425°F.

To make the tempeh marinade, combine the tamari, Bragg's, miso and water in a bowl big enough to accommodate the tempeh. Whisk vigorously until the miso has broken down and is evenly distributed. Gently coat each strip of the tempeh and marinate at room temperature for 20 minutes (minimum 10 minutes).

Grease a baking sheet with coconut oil. Place the marinated tempeh on the baking sheet, making sure to leave space between each slice.

Place the baking sheet in the oven. After 15 minutes, check the colour. If the bottoms are already dark brown and crispy-looking, turn each one over and let them bake for another 15 minutes. If the bottom is not yet dark brown and crispy, leave the tempeh on the tray on the same side for another 5 minutes, then check again and turn over. Tempeh is finished when both sides are brown and crispy, a total cooking time of about 30 minutes.

While the tempeh is cooking, prepare the taco filling by heating 1 teaspoon olive oil in a hot pan or wok over medium heat. Add three-quarters of the green onions and the garlic and ginger and sauté for 5 minutes, until the onions have softened. Stir often. Add the mushrooms to the pan with the Bragg's. Cook off the liquid, about 5 minutes. Mushrooms should brown slightly.

(RECIPE CONTINUES)

3 medium-large portobello mushrooms, stems removed, rubbed clean, thinly sliced

1 teaspoon Bragg's Liquid Aminos

12 small soft-shelled tortillas (use corn tortillas if gluten free is required)

½ cup finely chopped purple cabbage, for garnish

1 ripe avocado, sliced into thin wedges, for garnish

6 radishes, thinly sliced into rounds or matchsticks, for garnish

½ bunch cilantro, coarsely chopped, for garnish

1 tablespoon sesame seeds, for garnish

1 cup enoki mushrooms, rinsed and ends chopped off, for garnish

Juice of 3 limes

Prepare each taco by smearing about 1 tablespoon umami sauce on each tortilla. Place a strip of tempeh down the middle, then add several mushroom slices, some grated cabbage, a slice of avocado, some sliced radishes, a pinch of chopped cilantro, a sprinkle of sesame seeds, a few raw enoki mushrooms and some chopped raw green onions. Squeeze some lime juice overtop and serve immediately.

PRO TIP

Tamari is a category of Japanese soy sauce made with little to no wheat. Look for a gluten-free label if you are gluten intolerant. Bragg's Liquid Aminos is a liquid protein concentrate derived from soybeans. It is an excellent alternative (or addition) to tamari or soy sauce.

Lentils and Brown Rice with Rainbow Chard, Roasted Carrots and Tahini

Serves 4 to 6

This is our take on *mujaddara*, a classic Middle Eastern dish of rice and lentils garnished with caramelized onions. We've added rainbow chard and roasted carrots with tahini sauce to round out the meal. As alternatives or additions to the tahini sauce, this is excellent served with Warm Beet Hummus (page 99), Roasted Eggplant Dip (page 100) or some broken-up feta. Though this recipe asks for many pots and pans, each step is very simple. We like to make a big batch; this dish tastes great the next day, warmed up or served at room temperature.

MUJADDARA AND CARROTS

5 tablespoons virgin olive oil, divided

3 large white or yellow onions, peeled and sliced lengthwise into ¼-inch strips

1 bunch medium carrots, unpeeled, trimmed and scrubbed

1½ teaspoons sea salt, divided

1 teaspoon sweet paprika

2 teaspoons za'atar, divided

1½ cups short-grain brown rice

5¼ cups filtered water, divided

2 cloves garlic, peeled, divided

1½ cups brown lentils

5 leaves rainbow chard (small bunch), chopped in ribbons (4 loosely packed cups)

2 tablespoons finely chopped flat-leaf parsley, plus an extra sprig for garnish

2 tablespoons finely chopped fresh mint

1 tablespoon freshly squeezed lemon juice

½ cup black olives (preferably Moroccan cured), pitted

Pinch of sumac

Preheat the oven to 400°F. Line a baking sheet with parchment paper and set aside.

Warm a large pan over medium heat and add 3 tablespoons olive oil and the sliced onions. Sauté the onions on medium for 5 minutes, stirring to keep them from burning, then turn heat down to low and allow them to caramelize for 45 minutes, stirring every 5 to 7 minutes. Don't let them blacken. If they begin to stick to the pan, add ¼ cup water to deglaze. The onions are ready when they are sweet-smelling and caramel brown.

Place the carrots on the prepared baking sheet (leaving lots of space between them), and rub them with 1 tablespoon olive oil, a pinch of salt and paprika. Roast for about 45 minutes, checking every 15 minutes to move them around with a wooden spoon or spatula so every side gets evenly cooked. Roast until the outsides are well done and the insides are soft. Taste to determine readiness. Finish with a pinch of za'atar.

Meanwhile, prepare the rice and lentils. Rinse the rice under cold water. In a medium pot, combine rice, 2 cups water, a pinch of salt and 1 peeled garlic clove. Bring to a boil, cover and reduce heat to a simmer. Taste after 25 minutes. The rice is done when it's still a bit chewy but not hard. Mash the garlic clove against the side of the pot and mix through the rice. Set aside with the lid on.

Rinse the lentils under cold water, removing any bad guys. Cover them with 3 cups water in a large pot and add ½ teaspoon salt and the second peeled garlic clove. Bring to a boil, reduce heat and let simmer with the lid on. As with the rice, you want the lentils to be firm and to retain their shape. They're undercooked if they have a crunch when chewed;

(RECIPE CONTINUES)

TAHINI SAUCE

6 tablespoons filtered water

2 cloves garlic, minced

1 tablespoon freshly
squeezed lemon juice

3 tablespoons tahini

they're overcooked if they're mushy. Check after 15 minutes, and often thereafter. When the lentils are ready, drain away any remaining water. Set aside with the lid on.

Heat the remaining 1 tablespoon olive oil over medium heat, then add the chard. Sauté for 8 to 10 minutes, stirring often and adding a pinch of salt and 1 to 2 tablespoons water.

To make the tahini sauce, in a small pot over low heat, whisk together the water, garlic, lemon juice and tahini. Add additional water if it's too thick. Stir often. Keep it warm, but don't let it boil. As it cools, the sauce tends to separate; give it a swirl over heat right before serving.

Add the cooked rice to the pot with the lentils and warm over low heat. Add the sautéed chard, the finely chopped parsley and mint, lemon juice and a big pinch of za'atar. Stir to distribute evenly. Taste and adjust seasonings, if necessary.

To serve, fill a wide, shallow serving dish or individual bowls with the lentils and rice. Top with the caramelized onions, whole roasted carrots, black olives, an extra pinch of za'atar and a pinch of sumac. Finish with a generous drizzle of tahini sauce and a few sprigs of parsley.

Spiralized Zucchini Mac and Cheese with Oat Crumb Crust

Serves 4

This is plant-based comfort food at its best. Developed by Tara Tomulka, the founder of Rawcology (a raw, vegan kitchen in Toronto), it spins a pile of healthy ingredients into crispy, gooey, nutrient-dense gold. If you've never spiralized before, don't be daunted. There are many different kinds of spiralizers on the market, from the very simple to the very sophisticated. Ours is as simple as they come—it looks like a doll's hat and works like a manual pencil sharpener. You can also spiralize by making thin strips with a potato peeler. Or, if you're not in the mood to make noodles out of vegetables, you can make this dish with the pasta of your choice.

MAC AND CHEESE

½ cup raw cashews, soaked (see page 216)

½ cup raw Brazil nuts, soaked (see page 216)

4 medium zucchini

½ to 1 cup filtered water, divided

1 tablespoon Dijon mustard

2 cloves garlic

3 tablespoons nutritional yeast

1 tablespoon virgin olive oil

1 tablespoon freshly squeezed lemon juice

1 teaspoon ground turmeric

1 teaspoon apple cider vinegar

½ teaspoon sea salt

OAT CRUMB CRUST

½ cup gluten-free rolled oats

1 tablespoon virgin olive oil

Pinch of sea salt, for garnish

Pinch of freshly ground black pepper, for garnish

Fresh parsley or basil, for garnish

Turn on your oven's broiler, or preheat the oven to 400°F.

Cut the ends off your zucchini. We like to leave them unpeeled, but you can peel them if you'd prefer. Using a spiralizer, create zucchini "noodles." Place them in a large bowl and set aside.

To make the cheesy sauce, combine the cashews, Brazil nuts, ½ cup water, mustard, garlic, nutritional yeast, olive oil, lemon juice, turmeric, apple cider vinegar and salt in a blender or food processor and blend until smooth. If the sauce is too thick, slowly add the remaining ½ cup water until you have reached a smooth, sauce-like consistency. Taste and adjust seasoning if desired. Pour the sauce into the noodle bowl and mix until well coated.

To make the oat crumb crust, combine the oats and the olive oil in a food processor and pulse until well crumbled.

Arrange saucy noodles in a shallow baking dish and cover with a layer of the oat crumb crust. Broil until golden and warm all the way through. Garnish with salt, black pepper and a few leaves of parsley or basil.

Soba Noodles in Miso Broth with Daikon, Mushrooms and Crispy Tofu

Makes 4 to 6 bowls

Soba is the Japanese word for buckwheat. It is also used to describe long, thin, buckwheat noodles that are usually served either cold, with dipping sauce, or hot in a noodle soup. Buckwheat is often thought of as a grain, but in fact it is a fruit seed that is related to rhubarb. Buckwheat is gluten free (make sure your noodles are 100 percent buckwheat if you are gluten intolerant) and is rich in essential minerals and fibre. This is a great restorative soup for the wintertime; it's filling yet delicate, and extremely flavourful. Eat it with chopsticks and slurp the noodles noisily, the traditional way.

TOFU MARINADE

One 8-ounce package
extra-firm tofu

3 tablespoons tamari

1 tablespoon mirin

1 tablespoon toasted sesame oil

NOODLES

½ teaspoon sea salt

One 8-ounce package soba noodles (100% buckwheat or other varieties as preferred; kamut soba noodles are great, too)

FOR FRYING THE TOFU

¼ to ½ cup vegetable oil or coconut oil (depending on the size of your pan)

BROTH

1 onion, peeled and finely sliced

2 tablespoons virgin olive oil, divided

2 cups shiitake mushrooms or 2 large portobello mushrooms, stems removed, rubbed clean, thinly sliced

Pinch of sea salt

4 large carrots, peeled and thinly chopped

2 teaspoons peeled, grated fresh ginger (knob of about 1½ inches × ½ inch)

Begin by marinating the tofu. Dry the tofu in paper towel or clean kitchen towels, pressing it down gently to release its water. Change towels and repeat. Cut the tofu into small rectangular pieces. In a medium bowl, combine the tamari, mirin and sesame oil. Add the tofu and marinate at room temperature for about 30 minutes.

To cook the soba noodles (this can be done in advance), fill a medium pot with water, add a pinch of salt, cover and bring to a boil. When the water is boiling, place the soba noodles in the pot, stirring with a wooden spoon to keep the noodles from sticking together. Continue cooking, uncovered, for as long as the package recommends or until al dente.

While the noodles are cooking, prepare a large ice bath with ice cubes and cold water. Once the noodles are perfectly al dente, strain out the boiling water and immediately place the noodles in the ice bath. Alternatively, you can place the noodle-filled colander under the tap and run the coldest water you can get over the noodles for about 1 minute. The noodles will quickly become cool enough to handle; using your hands, "scrub" the noodles to rub off excess starch and ensure that all are being exposed to the cold water or ice. The cold water will stop the noodles from overcooking and ensure they don't stick together. Set cooked noodles aside.

When you're ready to cook the tofu (this can also be done in advance), heat the vegetable oil or coconut oil in a pan. The oil should be about ⅛ inch deep. The oil is ready once it starts to bubble a little. Drop the tofu in the oil carefully (keep the marinade nearby), and don't stir or touch it. After 1 to 2 minutes, turn the tofu. Repeat until it is crispy on all sides. Remove from the pan and place on a paper towel–lined plate to dry. When the tofu is dry, place it back in the marinade bowl. Reserve to put into soup.

(RECIPE CONTINUES)

9 cups filtered water

¼ large daikon (about 6 ounces), sliced in half lengthwise and thinly sliced into half circles, or 3 to 4 radishes, thinly sliced

1 tablespoon toasted sesame oil

1 tablespoon mirin

1 tablespoon tamari

2 teaspoons Bragg's Liquid Aminos

4 tablespoons light miso paste

1 package dried seaweed sheets (at least 5 sheets), torn

1 teaspoon ground cayenne pepper (more or less to taste for heat preference)

1 bunch green onions, thinly sliced

3 teaspoons sesame seeds

To make the broth, in a large soup pot, sauté the onion in 1 tablespoon olive oil for 10 minutes on medium heat until it begins to soften and release its fragrance. Be careful not to let it burn.

While the onion is sautéing, prepare the mushrooms. Warm the remaining 1 tablespoon olive oil in a frying pan or wok on medium heat. Add the chopped mushrooms, cover the pan and cook for about 4 minutes, stirring occasionally. Remove the lid and cook for another minute, or until all of the liquid evaporates. Add a pinch of salt and set aside.

When the onion is ready, add the carrots to the soup pot and sauté for 3 minutes, stirring often. Add the grated ginger and sauté for another minute, then add the water and daikon and bring to a boil. Once boiling, lower heat to simmer. Add the sesame oil, mirin, tamari and Bragg's Liquid Aminos. Turn off the heat and add the miso and half of the mushrooms. (It's best not to add the miso while the soup is cooking because the heat will kill off the beneficial enzymes in the miso.) Add 3 sheets of torn seaweed to the pot, along with the cayenne. Stir and taste. If you prefer more heat, add more cayenne, or you can add it individually when serving.

To serve, portion out the soba noodles and place a pile at the bottom of each bowl, then pour the broth overtop. Finish each bowl with a few of the remaining cooked mushrooms, 1 heaping tablespoon chopped green onions, ½ teaspoon sesame seeds, 4 to 6 pieces of tofu and ½ sheet of seaweed, either torn or whole. Serve with an extra pinch of cayenne or dash of tamari, if desired.

Very Veggie Curry with Exploded Yellow Lentils

Serves 4 to 6

This dish is inspired by Deeva and Lee's travels in southern India. It is not a heavy, creamy, saucy curry; it's the vegetables and spices that take centre stage. This curry need not be made with eggplant, cauliflower and okra; it can be made with any vegetables that are in season and speak to your condition. We call the yellow lentils "exploded" because we've slowly cooked them well beyond the point to which you might normally take them to create a protein- and fibre-rich yellow bed for our curry.

2 medium eggplants

1 head cauliflower

5 tablespoons coconut oil, divided

1 tablespoon cumin seeds

1 tablespoon fenugreek

1 tablespoon yellow mustard seeds

6 cloves garlic, peeled; mince 4 and leave 2 whole

2-inch piece fresh ginger, peeled and finely chopped

1-inch piece fresh turmeric, peeled and finely chopped, or 1 tablespoon ground turmeric

1-inch piece hot red chili pepper, seeded and finely chopped

2 medium white or yellow onions, diced

2 teaspoons sea salt, divided

10½ cups filtered water, divided

15 to 20 okra (about 2 cups chopped; optional)

2 cups yellow or orange split lentils

2 tablespoons hot curry powder

1 tablespoon garam masala

1 tablespoon hot paprika, plus extra for garnish

2 bay leaves

1 tablespoon tomato paste

Preheat the oven to 400°F. Line two baking sheets with parchment paper and set aside.

Start by preparing the eggplants and the cauliflower. Cut the eggplants into ¼-inch half moons or quarter moons. Remove the bottom 2 inches of the cauliflower stem. Cut the remaining stem into ½-inch-thick rounds and the head into small florets. Coat the cauliflower in 1 tablespoon coconut oil (you may need to warm it up to liquefy if it is solid) and place it on a prepared baking sheet. Coat the eggplant in 2 tablespoons coconut oil and spread it on the other baking sheet. Bake the cauliflower and eggplant for about 30 minutes, moving them around every 10 minutes. Remove the roasted vegetables once lightly browned and crispy on the outside and soft on the inside.

In a large skillet, toast the cumin, fenugreek and mustard seeds over low heat for 20 to 40 seconds until fragrant; watch carefully because they can burn fast. Once fragrant, add 1 tablespoon coconut oil and the chopped garlic, ginger, turmeric (unless using ground, which needs to be added later) and hot red chili. Sauté for 1 minute on low heat, then add the onions and ½ teaspoon salt. Sauté all together, stirring often, for 5 minutes at low heat; you don't want to fry this because the seeds can burn; you want to cook softly to release the flavours and eliminate some of the harshness of the whole seeds. The onions should get translucent. After 5 minutes, add water as needed (up to ½ cup) to avoid burning the pan; you want to keep the mixture moist. Continue cooking on the stovetop for another 15 to 20 minutes or until everything is soft. If you're cooking with okra (we love it, but the slippery texture is not for everyone), chop the okra on a severe diagonal into ⅛- or ¼-inch-thick slices. Add the okra to the curry pan and mix thoroughly. Cook for about 10 minutes.

(RECIPE CONTINUES)

½ cup finely chopped cilantro, plus extra leaves for garnish

2 limes, quartered, for garnish

While the curry is simmering, cook the lentils. Rinse the lentils, discard any bad guys, and add them to a medium pot with 6 cups water. Bring to a boil, boil for 1 full minute, then drain the water. Add the remaining 4 cups of water, 2 whole peeled garlic cloves and remaining ½ teaspoon salt. Bring the lentils back to a boil, then reduce heat to simmer with the lid on, skimming off foam and stirring often. Lentils are done after about 20 minutes, once they "explode" and almost all of the water has evaporated. You may need to strain the lentils to get the remaining water out. Add the remaining 1 tablespoon coconut oil and 1 teaspoon salt, then cover and set aside.

Add the roasted vegetables to the curry pan and stir in the hot curry powder, garam masala, paprika, bay leaves and tomato paste. (If you're not using fresh turmeric, add ground turmeric now.) Mix thoroughly and let the flavours mingle on low heat for another 5 to 10 minutes. If you prefer a sweeter curry, add another tablespoon of tomato paste. Taste for salt and adjust accordingly. Before serving, remove the bay leaves, add ¼ to ½ cup chopped fresh cilantro and stir. Garnish with extra cilantro leaves, an extra pinch of paprika and limes. Serve the curry on top of or beside exploded lentils.

This dish is great served alongside a sweet or savoury lassi (pages 210–213).

Amaranth-Stuffed Vine Leaves and Fava Purée with Onion Condiment

Makes about 25 rolls

Vine leaves, or dolmades, are a staple of several Mediterranean cuisines, but originally came from Turkey. They're usually stuffed with rice and sometimes with dried fruit. We've used amaranth, an ancient grain, because we like the finer texture. Be patient with yourself when learning how to roll the leaves. Jars of leaves often contain upwards of 50, so if your first 10 come out funny, don't despair; there are plenty more leaves in the jar. Just stick with it and you'll get it right. This one takes some time but is well worth the wait.

5 tablespoons virgin olive oil, divided

2 medium white onions, diced

1 large tomato, finely chopped

1 clove garlic, smashed

1½ cups amaranth

3 tablespoons chopped dill

1 tablespoon lemon zest

4 tablespoons freshly squeezed lemon juice, divided

2 teaspoons sea salt

½ teaspoon ground cayenne pepper

One 16-ounce jar grape/vine leaves packed in water

3 cups filtered water

Fava Purée with Onion Condiment (page 95)

In a large pan, heat 1 tablespoon olive oil over medium heat. Add the onions and sauté for 5 minutes. Add the tomatoes and sauté for another 3 minutes, stirring often. Add the garlic and sauté for another minute. Then add the amaranth, 3 tablespoons olive oil and the dill. Mix thoroughly. Add the lemon zest, 2 tablespoons lemon juice, the salt and the cayenne and mix thoroughly again. Remove from heat.

Remove the vine leaves from the jar, being careful not to rip them. Rinse the leaves in cold water. You don't have to dry them. To stuff the vine leaves, hold one leaf in the palm of your hand or place it on a cutting board or plate, shiny/smooth side down. Add 1 heaping tablespoon of amaranth mix just above the stem at the base of the leaf. Fold the right and left sides of the leaf closest to the base, perpendicular to the central vein. Then begin rolling the leaf from the base up, keeping the folded parts tucked in. Continue rolling, keeping the tucked parts tight, folding in the remaining leaf tips as you roll. It may take a few leaves to get the hang of it. Once each leaf is rolled, place on a large plate with the tip of the leaf on the bottom so it won't unravel. Try to use leaves without major holes or rips. Continue rolling until the mix is done.

Line the bottom and sides of a medium pot with one layer of extra vine leaves (here's a use for the torn ones). This is important, as it will ensure that your stuffed vine leaves don't burn. Carefully place the stuffed vine leaves on top of the leaves lining the pot, seam side down so they're held in place. Lay them tightly together so they don't come apart. Once you've filled the bottom with stuffed vine leaves, continue placing the rest on top of the first layer, beginning at the edges. Once all the stuffed vine leaves are in the pot, cover with water (approximately 3 cups) and add the remaining 1 tablespoon olive oil and remaining 2 tablespoons lemon juice.

(RECIPE CONTINUES)

Find a sturdy, upside-down plate that can withstand heat or a lid that will fit inside the pot, and sit it on top of the vine leaves, holding them tightly in place. Now cover the pot with its actual lid, bring to a boil and reduce heat to a simmer. Simmer, covered, for 45 minutes. Remove the lid and continue to simmer with the plate in place for about another hour and 15 minutes (total of about 2 hours) until all the water has evaporated. Once the water is all gone, turn off the heat and let sit for a minimum of 15 minutes before serving.

Serve at room temperature with Fava Purée and Onion Condiment. The stuffed vine leaves will last for a few days in the fridge, and often taste even better the next day when all the flavours have sunk in and the leaves have tightened.

Fava Purée with Onion Condiment

Makes about 6 servings

This is made with puréed yellow split peas (not to be confused with fava beans) and is a classic Greek dish. The purée makes a great dip for the vine leaves, but also works as an accompaniment to a range of other dishes. Think of it as a lighter, Greek version of hummus.

FAVA PURÉE

2 cups dry yellow split peas

7 cups filtered water, divided

2 teaspoons sea salt

2 bay leaves

1 yellow onion, peeled and halved

2 cloves garlic, peeled and halved

Virgin olive oil and sprig of dill or parsley, for garnish

ONION CONDIMENT

2 cups filtered water

1 medium white onion, peeled and coarsely chopped

1½ tablespoons sumac

1½ tablespoons virgin olive oil

1 teaspoon chopped flat-leaf parsley

Rinse the split peas and place them in a medium pot with 3 cups water. Bring to a boil and let boil for 3 minutes. Drain the water. (This step is important for ease of digestion!)

Return the split peas to the pot. Add the remaining 4 cups water, the salt, the bay leaves, the onion and the garlic. Bring to a boil on high, then turn burner to low and let simmer, covered, for 1 hour, stirring every 15 to 20 minutes or so. After 1 hour, mash the onion and garlic into the fava and taste for salt. Remove from heat and set aside, covered.

While the fava is cooking, prepare the onion condiment. Boil 2 cups water. Place the chopped onion in a mixing bowl. Prepare an ice bath in another mixing bowl with cold water and ice cubes. Pour the boiling water over the onion and let it sit for 30 seconds. Drain the hot water using a strainer or colander and place the onions in the ice bath for 2 minutes, then drain again. Leave the onions in the strainer for a few minutes, or set them on a piece of paper towel to dry. Place the onions in a dry bowl and add the sumac, olive oil and parsley. Serve the onion condiment on top of the fava or on the side.

Serve the fava dip warm with a drizzle of olive oil and a sprig of dill or parsley. Fava is best eaten as soon as it's ready (unlike the vine leaves). If you are making it ahead of time, add a small amount of water and olive oil to rehydrate it when reheating. It will keep for a few days in the fridge in a sealed container.

Bites

Warm Beet Hummus

Makes about 2 cups

This variation on one of our favourite themes is a great way to bring colour to your table. It can be made in a blender or food processor, but we recommend using a blender for the creamiest texture—and eating it right away, while it is still warm. We like to serve this smeared on a plate with some roasted vegetables or sliced green olives arranged overtop.

1 beet, stem removed, scrubbed, sliced in half

¾ cup filtered water, divided

1 garlic bulb, ¼ inch of top sliced off to expose cloves

1¾ cups cooked or canned chickpeas (see pro tip)

½ cup freshly squeezed lemon juice, plus more for garnish

2 tablespoons tahini

1 teaspoon sea salt

Sprig of parsley, for garnish

Drizzle of virgin olive oil

Pinch of za'atar, for garnish

Preheat the oven to 425°F.

Place the sliced beet in a rimmed baking dish or cast-iron skillet, sliced side down. Add ½ cup water. Wrap aluminum foil tightly overtop the baking vessel, sealing it. This will allow the beet to simultaneously roast and steam. Wrap the garlic bulb in aluminum foil and place it directly on a rack in your oven. Roast until the beet and garlic cloves are soft, about 25 minutes. Remove from oven and set aside to cool.

Cut the cooked beet into quarters and place it in the blender. Squeeze out two roasted garlic cloves from the skin (reserving the rest for another use) and add them to the blender with the chickpeas, lemon juice, tahini, salt and remaining ¼ cup water. Blend on high until very smooth. Taste and adjust flavour and consistency if needed. Serve warm or at room temperature, garnished with a sprig of parsley, an additional squeeze of lemon juice, a drizzle of olive oil and a pinch of za'atar. Store in an airtight container in the fridge for up to 3 days.

PRO TIP

If you are starting with dried rather than canned chickpeas, which we recommend, place dried chickpeas in a bowl and cover them with plenty of filtered water. Leave them to soak at room temperature overnight. Discard any chickpeas that float to the top. Rinse them well and transfer to a medium pot. Cover in water once again, add a teaspoon of salt, cover and bring to a boil. Reduce heat and simmer, covered, for about an hour. They are done when they have lost their hardness but are not yet mushy. Drain the cooking liquid, reserving some to use instead of filtered water in the hummus, and let the chickpeas cool.

Roasted Eggplant Dip

Makes about 1 cup

Inspired by the traditional Middle Eastern appetizer *mutabbal* or *baba ghanoush* made from mashed, roasted eggplant, this dip is one of our favourite snacks. We can't get enough of its deep, smoky flavour. You can serve it *mezze*-style with Warm Beet Hummus (page 99) and Raw Carrot Chipotle Dip (page 104), alongside the Lentils and Brown Rice (page 79), alongside or instead of the tahini sauce or as a light lunch with a bowl of warm pita and a green salad.

1 whole head garlic, ¼ inch of top sliced off to expose cloves

1 large eggplant or 2 medium eggplants

⅓ cup tahini

⅛ cup filtered water

3 tablespoons freshly squeezed lemon juice

½ teaspoon dried cumin

1 teaspoon freshly ground black pepper

2 tablespoons chopped flat-leaf parsley, plus extra sprigs for garnish

1 tablespoon virgin olive oil

¼ teaspoon sea salt, or more to taste

1 teaspoon sumac, for garnish

Preheat the oven to 425°F.

Wrap the garlic bulb in aluminum foil and place it in the oven. Roast until the cloves are soft, about 25 minutes. Remove from oven and set aside.

Meanwhile, poke the skin of your eggplant on all sides with a fork or a knife. This allows the steam to escape as it cooks and avoids an eggplant explosion. To roast the eggplant, turn on your oven's broiler, place the eggplant on a baking sheet lined with aluminum foil, and broil each side for about 2 minutes, until darkened. Reduce oven heat to 400°F. Bake the eggplant for about 30 minutes, or until very soft inside. Remove it from the oven and let it cool.

Once the eggplant is cool enough to handle, remove the skin and discard it. Place the flesh in a blender with the tahini, water, lemon juice, three cloves of roasted garlic (reserve the rest for future use), cumin, black pepper, parsley, olive oil and salt. Blend on medium for about 30 seconds, or until your desired consistency is reached. Taste and adjust if necessary. Serve warm or at room temperature, garnished with a few sprigs of parsley and a sprinkle of sumac. Store in an airtight container in the fridge for up to 3 days.

VARIATION

BARBEQUE EGGPLANT / For optimal smokiness, we like to poke holes in the eggplant and grill it over an outdoor fire or barbeque, turning it often with fire-safe tongs, until the exterior is black and the inside is very soft.

Sundried Tomato Tapenade

Makes about 1 cup

Tapenade has a strong personality. Few ingredients inspire as vehement a love-or-hate reaction as wrinkly black olives and anchovies, two usual suspects in the salty Provençal paste. To make ours extra controversial, we've added another acquired taste: sundried tomatoes, which bring a touch of sweetness. If you can't stand sundried tomatoes and prefer to replace them with a handful of capers or a salty little fish, more power to you! We love to spread a thin layer of this divisive dip onto warm Socca (page 66), Scottish Oatcakes (page 107) or Flax Crackers with Black Olives (page 108).

3 cloves garlic, peeled

½ cup Kalamata olives, pitted

½ cup sundried tomatoes (from a jar)

3 heaping tablespoons coarsely chopped flat-leaf parsley

2½ tablespoons virgin olive oil

2 tablespoons freshly squeezed lemon juice

2 tablespoons filtered water

Pinch of freshly ground black pepper

In a food processor or blender, combine the garlic, olives, sundried tomatoes, parsley, olive oil, lemon juice, water and pepper. Blend on low for 10 seconds, then increase the speed slowly to high. If you prefer a more rustic tapenade, stop before it's completely blended. Taste and adjust. If you like it smooth, you may wish to add a tablespoon of water or a bit more olive oil to get the appropriate texture. Store in a sealed jar in the fridge for about a week.

Raw Carrot Chipotle Dip

Makes about 1 cup

Our friend Tara Tomulka, a raw chef and holistic nutritionist, developed this delicious recipe. We were initially skeptical about the idea of including raw carrots and celery—which we tend to think of as vehicles for dip—in the dip itself. We then ate our words, as well as the entire bowl, with a few Scottish Oatcakes (page 107) and a spoon, spurred on by the touch of fiery chipotle and the hit of raw garlic potent enough to drive any vampire (or cold) away.

1 cup raw cashews, soaked
(see page 216)

3 medium carrots, peeled
and coarsely chopped

1 stalk celery, coarsely chopped

2 cloves garlic, peeled

¼ cup virgin olive oil

1 tablespoon freshly
squeezed lemon juice

1 teaspoon tamari or *nama
shoyu* (raw soy sauce)

1 teaspoon sweet paprika

½ teaspoon sea salt, or to taste

Pinch of chipotle chili flakes,
plus more for garnish

Drain and rinse the soaked cashews. Combine all ingredients in a food processor or blender and blend until smooth.

Serve chilled or at room temperature with a sprinkle of chipotle. Enjoy with crudités, Flax Crackers with Black Olives (page 108), Scottish Oatcakes (page 107) or a spoon. Keeps well in a sealed jar in the fridge for about 3 days.

Scottish Oatcakes

Makes 20 oatcakes

Scottish oatcakes are flaky, crumbly and wonderfully rich. They are also far easier to make than you would think. Traditionally, they are made with butter. We tried swapping in dearomatized coconut oil (which you can find online or in most well-stocked health food stores) and were astonished by how well it worked; the taste and texture are nearly identical. If you eat dairy, don't hesitate to replace the coconut oil with unsalted butter and serve these with a cheese plate and some onion relish. They're also excellent with Sundried Tomato Tapenade (page 103), Raw Carrot Chipotle Dip (page 104) or natural almond butter and a sprinkle of cinnamon.

1½ cups gluten-free rolled oats

⅔ cup brown rice flour (plus a bit more for rolling)

6 tablespoons dearomatized coconut oil, at room temperature

1 teaspoon sea salt

3 tablespoons cold filtered water

Preheat the oven to 350°F.

In a food processor, combine the rolled oats, brown rice flour, coconut oil and salt. Add the water slowly until the mixture comes together and starts to clump. The dough you end up with should hold together well.

Dust some extra flour onto a clean stretch of kitchen counter and onto a rolling pin. Push the dough into a ball and roll it out on the floured surface until it is ½ inch thick.

Using a glass or a round cookie cutter, cut the dough into rounds. Use a spatula to lift the rounds onto a lightly greased baking sheet. When you've cut out all the rounds you can fit, you can reroll the dough and cut some more. If it picks up too much flour and gets dry, add a touch more water.

Position the baking sheet in the centre of the oven and bake for 10 to 12 minutes, or until the oatcakes are browned a bit on the bottom. Remove from oven, let the oatcakes cool and enjoy. Store them in an airtight container. They will keep in your cupboard for a week or 10 days.

Flax Crackers with Black Olives

High in fibre and omega-3s, flax seeds have a lot going for them. Grinding them makes them more digestible and contributes to the crispiness of these crackers. You can grind whole flax seeds in an exceptionally clean coffee grinder and store extras in a sealed container in the fridge for use in smoothies. If black olives aren't your thing, you can certainly leave them out or substitute in a different accent. Scoring the half-baked giant cracker to create perfect squares is entirely optional; we prefer to just use our hands to break it apart into rustic-looking puzzle pieces once it's ready.

⅔ cup ground golden flax seeds

⅓ cup whole golden flax seeds

2 tablespoons raw pumpkin seeds

1 tablespoon raw sunflower seeds

1 teaspoon dried oregano

1 tablespoon nutritional yeast

3 tablespoons finely chopped, pitted black olives (about 8 olives, Moroccan cured or Kalamata)

1 clove garlic, minced

½ medium white onion, minced

1 cup filtered water

Preheat the oven to 350°F. Line a baking sheet with parchment paper and set aside.

Combine all ingredients in a large bowl. Mix thoroughly with your hands. Let sit at room temperature for 10 to 15 minutes until the mixture becomes gel-like.

Spread the dough out on the lined baking sheet until it is about ⅛ to ¼ inch thick, making sure there are no holes. Bake for 20 minutes, then remove the tray from the oven. With a sharp knife, score the partially baked giant cracker into 2-inch squares. Bake for another 20 minutes, then remove and flip. Bake for another 15 minutes, or until crispy.

Preserved Rainbow Peppers

Makes about 2 cups or one ½-quart jar

These smoky roasted peppers are the kind of thing you'll breathe a sigh of relief to find in your fridge when friends appear unexpectedly around cocktail hour and you didn't think you had anything to serve them with a glass of wine. They're perfect on a cracker, as part of an antipasti platter or all by themselves. We like to blacken our peppers over a grill on an outdoor fire; if you're going down that route, please remember: safety first. Otherwise these can be made in an oven, as described here.

4 to 6 red, orange and yellow bell peppers, sliced in half, cored and seeded

¼ cup apple cider vinegar

3 cloves garlic, minced

1 to 1½ cups virgin olive oil, divided

1 teaspoon sea salt

2 tablespoons dried herbs (we use an even mix of oregano, parsley and basil)

Pinch of freshly ground black pepper

Preheat the oven to 400°F. Sterilize a sealable ½-quart glass jar, such as a mason jar (see pro tip).

Place the peppers on a baking sheet and roast for 45 minutes, turning occasionally to ensure they cook evenly.

When the peppers are cooked, remove from the oven. To make it easier to remove the skins, place the peppers into small paper bags, one or two per bag, and roll the tops of the bags closed, locking in the steam. Leave the peppers in the bags for 20 minutes, then remove and scrape away the skins using a serrated knife. Use a paper towel to clean the peppers inside and out.

Place the peppers into a bowl and cover with the apple cider vinegar. Stir in the minced garlic, 1 cup olive oil, salt, dried herbs and black pepper.

With clean tongs, place one of the peppers inside the sterilized jar and top with olive oil. Repeat until all the peppers are in the jar. Add up to an additional ½ cup olive oil to make sure all peppers are submerged. Seal the jar and refrigerate. Give the sealed red peppers about a week in the jar for all the flavours to marry. They will last for about 3 to 4 weeks in the refrigerator.

PRO TIP

It's important to start with a sterilized canning jar. Either run your glass jar and lid through a detergent-free dishwasher on the hottest setting or fill a large pot with tap water and bring to a simmer. You do not want the water to come to a full boil. Lower the jar right side up into the pot of water. Leave it in the hot water, simmering with about an inch of water covering the jar, for 10 minutes. After 10 minutes, remove with tongs and let dry on clean kitchen towels. Do the same with the sealing ring and top of the jar. Immediately fill with red peppers and store in the fridge.

Hot, Crispy Chickpeas

Makes about 1 cup

These crispy chickpeas are great tossed into a salad or eaten straight, popcorn-style. We love the spicy tang of the chipotle-coriander-lime seasoning, but they're also excellent just seasoned with some salt. They taste the best when they're fresh out of the oven. Over time, they become starchy and lose their pop.

1¾ cups cooked or canned chickpeas (see pro tip, page 99)

2 tablespoons plus 3 teaspoons virgin olive oil, divided

2 teaspoons chipotle powder

1 teaspoon dried coriander

1 clove garlic, peeled, smashed and minced

½ teaspoon sea salt, plus more for garnish

½ tablespoon chopped fresh cilantro, for garnish

Wedge of lime, for garnish

Preheat the oven to 400°F. Line a baking sheet with parchment paper and set aside.

Dry the chickpeas thoroughly in a clean kitchen towel or paper towel. It's very important that no water remains, for the sake of crispiness. In a mixing bowl, massage 2 tablespoons olive oil into the chickpeas with your hands, making sure each one is coated. Stir in the chipotle, coriander, garlic and salt.

Spread the chickpeas on the lined baking sheet, with plenty of room around each chickpea so they can crisp up without cramping each other's style. Bake for 20 minutes, stirring once with a wooden spoon or spatula halfway through.

Take the chickpeas out of the oven and drizzle them with an additional 2 teaspoons olive oil. Turn the oven to broil and place the chickpeas back in, broiling for 3 to 5 minutes. Let them cool a bit, then try one. They're ready once they crackle or pop in your mouth. If they're not there yet, add the remaining 1 teaspoon olive oil and leave in the oven to broil for a few more minutes.

Garnish with cilantro, a tiny pinch of salt and the juice of a wedge of lime.

Baked Brassica Bites

Makes about 4 cups

Brassica is a genus of nutritionally high-achieving plants that includes kale, Brussels sprouts, cabbage, broccoli, cauliflower, rapini and bok choy. They are the Royal Tenenbaums of vegetables. Brassicas are extremely healthy, offering tons of vitamin C (among other antioxidants) and plenty of fibre. We've chosen just a few of our favourite brassicas, but feel free to use any member of the family for this snack.

1 head broccoli, florets cut into bite-sized pieces and stems peeled and cut into ¼-inch coins

1 head cauliflower, cut like the broccoli

15 Brussels sprouts, hard, dark bases removed and the sprouts halved

2 tablespoons virgin olive oil

1 teaspoon sea salt

Pinch of freshly ground black pepper

2 sprigs rosemary, leaves torn or chopped and stems discarded

½ teaspoon sweet paprika

Preheat the oven to 400°F. Line two baking sheets with parchment paper and set aside.

In a large mixing bowl, toss the broccoli, cauliflower and Brussels sprouts with the olive oil, salt, black pepper, rosemary and paprika. Mix until evenly distributed.

Spread the brassica mixture on the baking sheets. You don't want the veggies touching; they need space to get crispy. (You may need to do this in two batches.) Place them in the oven and roast for 30 to 40 minutes, moving them around occasionally, until they are crispy and evenly browned.

These veggies taste incredible fresh out of the oven. They lose their crunch over time or once stored in the fridge, but still taste great. They also work well as a side dish or added to a green salad.

Za'atar Kale Chips

Makes 4 cups

If you thought kale chips were getting a bit tired, try them with some za'atar. A popular spice blend in the Levant, it usually contains thyme, sesame seeds, marjoram, oregano, sumac and salt. You should be able to find it in the spice section of a well-stocked grocery store. If you can't, and if you don't have a spice shop or Middle Eastern grocery store close by, you can buy it online. It's well worth a hunt. We like to sprinkle it on top of a bowl of hummus, on a warm pita rubbed with olive oil or on roasted vegetables.

4 cups curly kale, dried thoroughly

1 tablespoon virgin olive oil

1 teaspoon za'atar, plus more to taste

Pinch of sea salt (only if your za'atar mix doesn't contain salt)

Preheat the oven to 400°F. Line two baking sheets with parchment paper and set aside.

De-stem the kale leaves by holding the bottom of the stem in one hand and using your other hand to pull the leaf off the stem in one smooth motion. Then coarsely chop or tear the leaves into bite-sized pieces.

Place the kale in a large mixing bowl with the olive oil. Massage the olive oil into the leaves with your hands. Add 1 teaspoon za'atar and distribute evenly. Add the salt if your za'atar mix doesn't already contain salt. Then spread the kale on the two baking sheets, being careful not to overcrowd the leaves. You may need to do this in two batches.

Bake for 8 to 10 minutes, mixing the kale around with a wooden spoon or spatula at the 4-minute mark.

Top with an extra pinch of za'atar and serve immediately.

Chia Seed Chai Energy Bars

Makes 12 bars

These are some of the best energy bars we've ever tasted. We've tried crispy ones, crumbly ones, chewy ones and gooey ones, and we promise none are as good as these. They were invented by Brooke Lundmark, a holistic nutritionist and Greenhouse team member. We like to make a huge batch and store them in the freezer. They're delicious when they're still nice and cold with a bit of bite, and equally spectacular wrapped in parchment paper and slipped into your bag, to be discovered a few hours later, just when you need a boost.

2 cups gluten-free rolled oats

4 tablespoons chia seeds

2⅓ cups natural almond butter

10 Medjool dates, pitted

5 tablespoons coconut butter

½ cup Brazil nuts

½ teaspoon sea salt

½ teaspoon ground coriander

½ teaspoon ground cloves

½ teaspoon ground cardamom

1 tablespoon ground cinnamon

1 tablespoon ground ginger

TOPPINGS

Goji berries (optional)

Unsweetened coconut flakes (optional)

Chia seeds (optional)

Combine all ingredients in a food processor. Pulse until well combined and starting to form a ball.

Press the mixture into an 8-inch square pan and flatten with a piece of parchment paper. You can top the bars with chopped goji berries, coconut flakes, chia seeds, spices or the decorative garnish of your choice. Press them down again with parchment paper and chill for an hour in the fridge or freezer before cutting into bars and serving.

These will keep well in the fridge for about a week or in the freezer for about a month.

Naked Almonds

Makes 4 cups

Our friend Teresa Ayson invented this beautifully simple snack. The slow roasting gives these almonds a golden tan and the perfect degree of crunch. It also brings out their natural sweetness and fills the house with a delicious smell. Just don't forget about them! Almonds are nutritious and satisfying, and snacking on a handful of these with a green juice in the mid-afternoon is a great way to maintain your energy levels, whether you're working late or striving for an early evening workout. We keep a big glass jar of them on the kitchen counter at all times.

4 cups raw almonds

5 cups boiling filtered water

Preheat the oven to 250°F.

Place the almonds in a heat-safe bowl and cover them in the boiling water. Allow them to soak for about 30 minutes as the water cools. When it is cool enough to handle, use your hands to peel off the skins. The hot water loosens them, making them easier to remove. If they're being stubborn, allow the almonds to soak for another 15 minutes and try again.

Dry the peeled almonds using a clean kitchen towel or paper towel. Spread them out in a single layer on baking sheets, allowing for space between each one. You may need to do this in batches.

Roast the almonds for 3 hours, shuffling them around with a wooden spoon every 30 minutes to an hour to ensure that they roast evenly.

When the almonds are perfectly golden, remove them from the oven and allow them to cool. Store in a sealed jar at room temperature. They keep for a few weeks.

Hangry Bites

When spoken in English by someone with a French accent, the words "hungry" and "angry" sound very similar. We don't think this is a coincidence. For many of us, the lower the blood sugar, the shorter the fuse. Instead of letting ourselves get hangry in the middle of the afternoon (which can lead to doing and saying things we regret), we do our best to have energizing bites like these on hand.

Blueberry Lemon Bites

Makes 12 to 14 bites

1 cup gluten-free rolled oats

1 cup unsweetened coconut flakes, plus extra for rolling

½ cup hemp seeds

½ cup dried blueberries

½ cup natural almond butter

1 tablespoon coconut oil

¼ teaspoon sea salt

3 tablespoons lemon zest

1 tablespoon freshly squeezed lemon juice

3 tablespoons pure maple syrup

In a food processor, pulse all ingredients until well combined. Form into 1- to 2-inch balls and roll them in coconut flakes. Store in the fridge for up to a week or in the freezer for about a month.

Double Cacao Protein Bites

Makes 12 to 14 bites

¼ cup coconut oil

1½ cups leftover fibre from Almond Milk (page 219) or any nut or seed milk fibre, or rolled oats pulsed in a food processor

½ cup raw cacao powder, plus extra for rolling

½ cup unsweetened coconut flakes

1 teaspoon spirulina

2 Medjool dates, pitted, or 2 tablespoons date paste (see Spiced Grain-Free Granola with Brazil Nut Fibre, page 45)

¼ cup pure maple syrup

¼ teaspoon sea salt

Warm the coconut oil on low heat until just melted. In a large bowl, mix all ingredients until well combined. Form into 1- to 2-inch balls and roll them in cacao powder. Store in the fridge for up to a week or in the freezer for about a month.

Desserts

Vanilla Bean Cheesecake with Coconut Whipped Cream

Makes one 10½-inch round cake, 10 to 12 slices

When it comes to decadent desserts that are filled with good things, we call upon Greenhouse alum Emily Kreeft. Emily is a nutritionist and our plant-based dessert authority. When she set her mind to creating a "cheesecake" that would be suitable for our friends with dairy sensitivities, we did not doubt for a second that it would be one of the best cheesecakes we had ever tasted. And it is. Top with coconut whipped cream and fresh berries for a cold, cloud-like slice of magic.

CRUST

2 cups Medjool dates, pitted and soaked in warm water for 15 minutes

2 cups raw almonds

1 teaspoon ground cinnamon

½ teaspoon sea salt

FILLING

2 cups raw cashews, soaked (see page 216)

⅔ cup coconut oil

1 cup canned full-fat coconut milk (we use Thai Kitchen)

6 vanilla beans, sliced lengthwise, seeds scraped out and reserved, or 2 tablespoons pure vanilla extract

⅔ cup pure maple syrup

2 tablespoons freshly squeezed lemon juice

COCONUT WHIPPED CREAM AND TOPPINGS

One 14-ounce can full-fat coconut milk (we use Thai Kitchen), refrigerated overnight

1 tablespoon powdered cane sugar or icing sugar

½ cup blueberries, for garnish

½ cup raspberries, for garnish

Shaved dark chocolate and chopped nuts, for garnish

To make the crust, add the dates to a food processor and blend on high until they form a paste. Scrape out the date paste and set aside.

Add the almonds to the food processor and pulse until pebble-like (not an almond meal consistency). Add the cinnamon, salt and dates, and blend until smooth.

Line a 10½-inch round springform pan with parchment paper cut to fit snugly in the bottom. Scoop the crust into the parchment-lined pan and press it down firmly with your hands until it reaches the edges and is even on top.

To make the filling, add the drained and rinsed cashews to a food processor. Pulse on high for 15 seconds. Add the coconut oil, coconut milk, vanilla seeds or extract, maple syrup and lemon juice, and blend on high for 1 minute, or until you can see and taste that the cashews are blended thoroughly. Pour the cashew mixture evenly over the crust, cover with plastic wrap and put into the freezer for 4 hours.

To make the coconut whipped cream, remove the can of coconut milk from the fridge, drain any of the coconut water off the top, put the solids into a bowl, and sift in the powdered cane sugar or icing sugar. With a hand mixer (or with a whisk and some elbow grease), whip on high until peaks form. This will yield roughly 1½ cups coconut whipped cream.

When ready to serve, remove the cheesecake from the freezer and top with a layer of whipped cream and some fresh blueberries and raspberries (if using), or the garnish of your choice. The cake keeps well in the freezer for up to 1 month.

PRO TIP

For an intense vanilla flavour, grind the seeds from inside the vanilla bean into a fine powder using a mortar and pestle. We use Prana raw whole vanilla beans, which you can find at health food stores or online.

Raspberry Tart with Pistachio Crust

Makes 2 round 6-inch tarts

With a pistachio crumb crust, a layer of rich cream and a pile of tart, juicy raspberries, this is a very special dessert. Lee Reitelman, who developed many of the savoury recipes in this book with his partner Deeva Green, invented it for Deeva's birthday. He was seeking to emulate a raspberry tart she requested every year for her birthday as a child. By all accounts, he may have surpassed it.

CRUST

½ cup shelled pistachios

½ cup almond flour

½ cup shredded, unsweetened coconut

2 tablespoons pure maple syrup

2 tablespoons vegetable oil

TOPPING

2 cups raw cashews, soaked (see page 216)

⅓ to ¾ cup filtered water

2 tablespoons pure maple syrup

½ vanilla bean, sliced lengthwise, seeds scraped out and reserved, or ½ teaspoon pure vanilla extract

1½ cup raspberries

6 shelled, smashed pistachios, for garnish (optional)

½ teaspoon freshly squeezed lemon juice, for garnish (optional)

1 mint leaf, for garnish (optional)

Icing sugar (for dusting)

Preheat the oven to 325°F.

To make the crust (this can be done up to 3 days in advance), grind the pistachios in a food processor for 30 seconds. The goal is to get a coarse grind, not a powder. With a fork, mix the pistachios with the almond flour, shredded coconut, maple syrup and oil until well combined. Divide the mixture in half. Press one half into a 6-inch tart pan. Aim for a thickness of about ¼ inch on the bottom and ½ inch at the walls. Do the same with the other half into a second pan.

Bake both crusts for 15 minutes. The edges will begin to darken; don't let them turn black. Take them out of the oven and allow them to cool for at least 30 minutes. Store them in the fridge or freezer if you are making them in advance.

To make the cream topping, combine the drained and rinsed cashews in a blender with ⅓ cup water, the maple syrup and vanilla seeds or extract. Blend on high for 30 to 45 seconds. You want to get a luxurious, silky cream with the consistency of pancake batter. If it's too thick, add a bit of water at a time until it is just right.

When the crusts are cool, spoon a generous layer of cashew cream into each one, using enough so that the cream is ¼ inch lower than the height of the pan. Arrange raspberries overtop both tarts. If using, top with crushed pistachios, lemon juice and/or mint (if using). Dust with icing sugar and serve.

Oatmeal Chocolate Chip Sea Salt Cookies

Makes 20 to 25 cookies

Cookies are quite possibly one of the best things on Earth. Emily Kreeft developed this gluten- and dairy-free variation on our favourite kind of cookie—oatmeal chocolate chip—and it is a definite party pleaser. To upgrade the chocolate chips to chocolate chunks, use a dark chocolate bar broken up into nice, big pieces that will turn gooey and melty in the oven.

1 cup coconut sugar

½ cup coconut oil

¼ cup Brazil Nut Milk (page 224) or Almond Milk (page 219)

1 tablespoon pure vanilla extract

2 cups gluten-free flour (we use Bob's Red Mill brand, or see pro tip)

1 teaspoon baking powder

1 teaspoon baking soda

1 teaspoon sea salt, plus more for garnish

1½ cups dairy-free chocolate chips or chocolate chunks

¾ cup gluten-free rolled oats

Preheat the oven to 350°F. Line a baking sheet with parchment paper and set aside.

In a medium bowl, cream together the coconut sugar and coconut oil, then slowly add the Brazil Nut Milk or Almond Milk and vanilla.

In another medium bowl, combine the flour, baking powder, baking soda and salt. Mix the wet and dry ingredients together in a food processor or using a hand mixer. Using a wooden spoon, fold in the chocolate chips and rolled oats.

Form cookies the size of golf balls and drop them onto the baking sheet. Using a fork, lightly pat down each cookie, then sprinkle some extra chocolate chips and a pinch of coarse salt on top. Bake for about 7 minutes. We like to underbake slightly for a chewy texture.

PRO TIP
Emily's Homemade Gluten-Free All-Purpose Flour

1½ cups brown rice flour

⅓ cup tapioca flour

½ cup sweet rice flour

½ cup potato starch

1 teaspoon xanthan gum

Combine all ingredients and store in a cool, dry place in a tightly secured container. The xanthan gum serves as a binding agent, which is a role normally played by gluten. You can forgo it, but if you do, your baked goods will have a crumblier texture.

Fall Fruit Crumble

Makes 6 to 8 servings

A warm dish of fruit crumble with a cold dollop of coconut whipped cream is the perfect dessert for early fall, when the air has just taken on a bit of a bite. But you don't have to wait until sweater weather to make this recipe—it also works well in the spring with rhubarb and strawberries. And if pears are not in season, you can make it with apples alone, using any variety of apple that grows close to you or a combination of your favourites.

FILLING

2 green apples, cored and sliced into ¼-inch half moons

2 pears (any variety), cored and sliced into ¼-inch half moons

3 tablespoons freshly squeezed lemon juice

¼ teaspoon ground nutmeg

½ teaspoon ground cinnamon

2 teaspoons coconut oil for greasing baking dish(es)

2 tablespoons filtered water

CRUMBLE

1 cup gluten-free rolled oats

½ cup brown rice flour

½ cup white rice flour

4 tablespoons pure maple syrup, divided

5 tablespoons coconut oil, just melted

¼ teaspoon sea salt

TOPPING

Dairy-free ice cream or coconut whipped cream (see page 140)

Preheat the oven to 400°F.

To make the filling, first place the apples and pears in a medium mixing bowl. Stir in the lemon juice, nutmeg and cinnamon, making sure the slices are well coated. Let them sit at room temperature for 10 to 20 minutes.

To make the crumble, in a separate medium mixing bowl, combine the oats, brown rice flour, white rice flour, 3 tablespoons maple syrup, the coconut oil and salt with your hands or a wooden spoon. The ingredients should stick together a little because of the coconut oil.

Grease the bottom and sides of a casserole dish or individual, oven-safe ramekins with coconut oil. Add the filling mixture and 2 tablespoons water to the dish (or distribute among all of the dishes). Cover evenly with crumble and drizzle the remaining 1 tablespoon maple syrup overtop. Cover the baking dish(es) loosely with aluminum foil and bake for 20 minutes. Remove aluminum foil after 20 minutes and continue baking for another 30 minutes or so, until fruit is soft and warm underneath and crumble has browned. Serve hot with your choice of dairy-free ice cream or coconut whipped cream.

Raw Dark Chocolate Bars with Fig Base

Makes 16 bars

Once you've added this simple recipe to your repertoire, you'll never look at a store-bought candy bar the same way. The soft and chewy fig, almond and coconut base pairs beautifully with the dark, rich layer of cacao laced with almond butter. We love adding some fig slices on top for a sweet bit of crunch.

FIG BASE

2 cups raw almonds

1 cup Medjool dates, pitted

½ cup dried figs

½ cup shredded, unsweetened coconut

½ teaspoon pure vanilla extract

CHOCOLATE LAYER

½ cup plus 1 tablespoon raw cacao powder

7½ tablespoons raw agave

3 tablespoons coconut oil

3 tablespoons natural almond butter

1 tablespoon pure vanilla extract

½ teaspoon sea salt

½ cup warm filtered water

TOPPINGS

Fig slices, coconut flakes, hemp seeds, almond slivers and coarse salt, for garnish

To make the fig base, first pulse the almonds into flour in a food processor. Add the dates, figs, coconut and vanilla, and blend until the mixture sticks together.

Line a 9-inch square pan (or a 13- × 9-inch pan for thinner bars) with parchment paper and press the base layer into the pan. Put it into the freezer while you get started on the chocolate layer.

To make the chocolate layer, blend the cacao powder, agave, coconut oil, almond butter, vanilla and salt in your food processor until smooth. Add the warm water slowly, either while the food processor is running (through the window in the top) or bit by bit.

Take the fig base out of the freezer and use a rubber spatula to spread the chocolate layer on top. Garnish with fig slices, coconut flakes, hemp seeds, almond slivers, coarse salt or the toppings of your choice.

Let the bars set in the freezer for 1 to 2 hours. You can take them out after 30 minutes or so to score them with a hot, wet knife to make them easier to cut. Serve directly out of the freezer or at room temperature. These bars will keep well in the freezer for about a month.

Apple Pecan Squares with Caramel Sauce

Makes 12 squares

Let's say you have part of a fall Sunday on your hands and you want to make something exceptional. Start with a batch of Almond Milk (page 219) and reserve the fibre to make these spicy, nutty squares drizzled with caramel sauce. You can then enjoy them with a glass of the Almond Milk—or, if you're feeling really ambitious, turn it into Almond Chai or Harvest Milk (page 245 or 232). The squares will last all week in the fridge or even longer in the freezer. You'll be thanking yourself well past Thanksgiving.

SQUARES

2 cups leftover fibre from Almond Milk (page 219) or any nut or seed milk fibre

2 cups unsweetened coconut flakes

½ cup whole flax seeds

1 cup pecans

¾ cup chopped dried apples

1 cup natural almond butter

½ cup coconut oil

3 vanilla beans, sliced lengthwise, seeds scraped out and reserved, or 1 tablespoon pure vanilla extract

6 tablespoons pure maple syrup

2 teaspoons ground nutmeg

1 tablespoon ground ginger

1 tablespoon ground cinnamon

CARAMEL SAUCE

1 cup coconut sugar

1 cup cold filtered water

1 cup canned full-fat coconut milk (we use Thai kitchen)

¼ teaspoon sea salt

4 vanilla beans, sliced lengthwise, seeds scraped out and reserved, or 4 teaspoons pure vanilla extract

For the squares, combine the Almond Milk fibre, coconut flakes, flax seeds, pecans, dried apples, almond butter, coconut oil, vanilla seeds or extract, maple syrup, nutmeg, ginger and cinnamon in a food processor. Blend until it all sticks together and forms a ball.

Scrape the mixture into an 8-inch square cake pan and press it down with a piece of parchment paper, flattening the top. Chill for an hour, then run a knife under hot water and score into squares.

For the caramel sauce, in a small saucepan, bring the coconut sugar and water to a boil on high heat. Stir gently until the sugar has melted, about 3 to 4 minutes. Reduce the heat to medium, add the coconut milk and stir until there are no lumps. Boil gently on medium for 12 to 15 minutes, until the sauce is dark amber and your desired consistency has been reached. Remove from heat and stir in the salt.

Add the vanilla seeds or extract to the cooling caramel sauce, giving it a good stir. Once it has fully cooled, pour the caramel sauce into a small mason jar and store in the refrigerator for up to 2 weeks.

Serve apple pecan squares cold or at room temperature, drizzled with caramel sauce. Store extra bars for up to a week in the fridge or up to a month in the freezer.

Sweet Potato Brownies

Makes 18 brownies

One of our favourite places to have lunch in Toronto is iQ FOOD CO., a collection of local restaurants developed and brilliantly executed by our friend Alan Bekerman and his brother Arthur. Geared toward busy people who like to eat well, iQ elevates perfectly cooked and thoughtfully arranged ingredients to an art form. Thanks to the extreme generosity of Alan, Arthur and Christine Flynn, iQ's talented head chef (also known as Chef Jacques La Merde), here is the recipe for one of iQ's most famous desserts: sweet potato brownies.

1 large sweet potato

1 cup plus 1 tablespoon natural almond butter

½ cup plus 1 tablespoon raw agave

1 cup unsweetened applesauce

3 teaspoons chia seeds

1½ cups unsweetened cocoa powder

⅔ cup dairy-free chocolate chips

2 teaspoons baking soda

¾ teaspoon sea salt

Blueberries, for garnish

Preheat the oven to 350°F.

Pierce the sweet potato all over with a fork to allow steam to escape while it is roasting. Position a piece of aluminum foil on the bottom of your oven and place the sweet potato directly on the rack above it. The foil will catch the dripping sweetness. Roast the sweet potato for 45 minutes, turning once. Once it is cool enough to handle, remove the skin and mash the flesh. This can be done in advance.

Reduce the heat to 325°F. Line a rimmed 9- × 9-inch baking dish with parchment paper.

In a large bowl, cream together the mashed sweet potato, almond butter, agave and applesauce. Make sure there are no lumps in the almond butter. Pour all dry ingredients on top. Combine with a rubber spatula. The trick is to eliminate the lumps but not to overmix. If you mix too much, the baking soda will activate early and the brownies won't rise.

Bake for 26 minutes, then remove from oven and let cool. Gently remove from dish, wrap tightly in plastic wrap and freeze. After about an hour, use a hot, wet knife to cut evenly into 18 brownies. Serve chilled or at room temperature. They are messy, but it's part of the fun.

Pumpkin Pie with Coconut Whipped Cream

Makes a 9-inch pie

Pumpkin pie doesn't really require an explanation, does it? This recipe is from Elena Mari, our former store manager and the talented artist and stylist who, along with her partner Nathan Legiehn, is responsible for the fact that you might be licking the adjacent page right now. Like every other recipe in this book, this pie is dairy free, gluten free and filled with things your body will give thanks for.

CRUST

¾ cup raw almonds

⅓ cup Medjool dates, pitted or dried figs

1 to 2 teaspoons pure vanilla extract

¼ cup shredded, unsweetened coconut

FILLING

1¾ cups pumpkin purée (you can roast a pumpkin and purée the flesh or use canned)

¼ cup melted coconut oil

¼ cup Almond Milk (page 219) or other non-dairy milk

1 teaspoon pure vanilla extract

1 teaspoon ground cinnamon

½ teaspoon pumpkin pie spice

¾ cup Medjool dates, pitted

COCONUT WHIPPED CREAM

One 14-ounce can full-fat coconut milk (we use Thai Kitchen), refrigerated overnight

1 teaspoon pure maple syrup

½ teaspoon pure vanilla extract

To make the crust, in a food processor, grind the almonds into flour. Add the dates or figs and vanilla and continue to grind until the dried fruit is broken down. If the mixture is too dry, add a teaspoon of water. Add the coconut and blend all crust ingredients. Press the crust into a 9-inch pie pan.

To make the filling, in a blender, combine the pumpkin, coconut oil, Almond Milk, vanilla, cinnamon and pumpkin pie spice. Blend until mixture becomes a liquid. Add the dates and mix until fully broken down. Once you have a smooth filling, pour it into the crust. Let the pie chill in the fridge for at least 4 hours before serving.

To make the coconut whipped cream, remove the can of coconut milk from the fridge, strain off the liquid and place the solids in a bowl. Use a hand mixer or a whisk and elbow grease to whip up the coconut cream, maple syrup and vanilla for 5 to 6 minutes or until it forms stiff peaks. Spoon coconut whipped cream onto your pumpkin pie, and enjoy!

Sticky Ginger Cake with Lemon Sauce

Makes an 8- × 12-inch cake (or a 9-inch round cake) and approximately 1½ cups lemon sauce

This is adapted from a Depression-era recipe labelled "My Best Gingerbread" by "Aunty Kay," the great-aunt of my mom's childhood best friend, which resides on a neatly printed cue card in my mom's family recipe file. I've been eating this warming cake around Christmastime for as long as I can remember. The original recipe contained butter, wheat flour, white sugar and a single egg—and feel free to make it that way if you'd like—but this version with coconut oil, rice flour and a flax "egg" is at least as good, if not even better.

GINGER CAKE

1 beaten flax "egg" (1 tablespoon ground flax seeds whisked with 3 tablespoons warm water)

½ cup coconut oil, at room temperature (solid)

½ cup coconut sugar

¾ cup molasses

2 tablespoons ginger juice or 1 tablespoon finely grated fresh ginger

2 cups white rice flour

1½ teaspoons baking soda

1½ teaspoons xanthan gum

1 teaspoon ground cinnamon

½ teaspoon ground cloves

½ teaspoon sea salt

½ to ¾ cup hot filtered water

1 teaspoon coconut oil, for greasing cake pan

LEMON SAUCE

½ cup coconut sugar

1 tablespoon cornstarch

1 cup filtered water

Zest of 1 lemon

¼ cup freshly squeezed lemon juice

Pinch of sea salt

3 tablespoons dearomatized coconut oil

Preheat the oven to 350°F.

To prepare the flax egg, in a small bowl whisk 1 tablespoon ground flax seeds into 3 tablespoons warm water. Let it sit for 10 minutes or longer, until it turns into a gel. The best version of this involves grinding your own flax seeds in a very clean coffee grinder (grind something else in between the coffee and the flax seeds and discard to ensure that all coffee residue is eliminated), but you can also buy pre-ground flax seeds—just make sure they're fresh.

In a large bowl, cream together the coconut oil and sugar with a hand mixer. Add the molasses, beaten flax "egg" and ginger. In a separate bowl, sift together the flour, baking soda, xanthan gum, cinnamon, cloves and salt. Add the dry ingredients to the wet ingredient bowl along with ½ cup hot water, and beat until smooth. Add a bit more hot water if you're not using ginger juice, or if the batter needs it to smooth out properly, up to ¾ cup in total.

Grease an 8- × 12-inch cake pan or a 9-inch round cake pan with coconut oil. Pour the batter into the pan and bake for 35 minutes, or until a toothpick inserted into the middle of the cake comes out clean.

For the lemon sauce, combine the coconut sugar and cornstarch in a saucepan. Stir in the water, lemon zest, lemon juice and a pinch of salt. Bring to a boil, stirring until thickened, about 10 minutes. Reduce to low and add dearomatized coconut oil, stirring until melted. Cool, and keep in fridge for up to 1 week. When you're ready to serve the cake, warm the lemon sauce in a small pan over low heat, stirring well. Drizzle or spread it on the cake, slice and serve.

Key Lime Cups

Makes about 8 mini cups

These offer a refreshing taste of summer in any season. We love making mini cups in shot glasses; they're the perfect bite when you need a little something sweet. These can also be made into a pie or tarts using the pie crust recipe from the Pumpkin Pie (page 140). Coconut whipped cream adds an extra layer of fluffy decadence.

2 ripe avocados, pitted

¾ cup freshly squeezed key lime juice (roughly 12 key limes or 6 limes)

½ cup raw agave

½ teaspoon pure vanilla extract

Pinch of sea salt

½ cup coconut oil

Coconut whipped cream (optional; see page 140)

Shredded, unsweetened coconut and lime zest, for garnish

In a food processor, combine the avocados, lime juice, agave, vanilla, salt and coconut oil until smooth. Pour into cups, glasses or small bowls.

Layer with coconut whipped cream, if desired. Chill in the fridge or freezer for at least 1 hour. Garnish with shredded coconut and lime zest, and serve.

Cups will keep well in the fridge for 2 to 3 days.

Chocolate Hemp Peanut Butter Balls

Makes 20 to 25 balls

This recipe came about as Easter was fast approaching and we were hunting for a healthier alternative to Easter eggs. These are indulgent and rich, but the protein and healthy fats from the hemp seeds and nut butter give them some staying power!

1½ cups natural crunchy peanut butter or natural almond butter

1 cup Medjool dates, pitted

1 tablespoon coconut oil

1 tablespoon filtered water

1 teaspoon pure vanilla extract

½ teaspoon sea salt

¾ cup brown rice crisp cereal

½ cup hemp seeds

1 cup dairy-free dark chocolate chips or your favourite dark chocolate bar, chopped

Line a baking sheet with parchment paper and set aside.

Spoon the nut butter into a food processor. We use crunchy because it adds to the heavy texture and helps to bind ingredients together. Add the dates, coconut oil, water, vanilla and salt and blend on high until the mixture forms a thick paste.

Put the brown rice crisps into a sealable bag and roll a canned good over the bag until the crisps break down into smaller pieces but remain bulky. (You don't want crumbs.) Using a wooden spoon, stir the brown rice crisps and hemp seeds into the nut butter paste.

In a double boiler, melt the chocolate chips. Form Ping-Pong-sized balls from the nut butter paste. Using a spoon, dip and roll each ball into the chocolate until it's coated, then spoon onto your lined baking sheet (or any stable flat surface that will fit in your freezer and can handle the cold). Once the baking sheet is full, place it in the freezer for 45 minutes.

Serve cold or at room temperature. These will keep well in the freezer for about a month.

Juices

Equipment

———

Here are four categories of juicing contraptions, along with their pros and cons. The recipes in this Juice section will work with all of these kinds of juicers. However, please be aware that taste, texture, produce yield and shelf life will vary depending on which type of juicer you are using and the ripeness of your ingredients.

Cold Presses

At Greenhouse, the juice we make is cold-pressed. Cold pressing is a method of extracting liquid from a plant using hydraulic pressure. The pros are that the juice that trickles out contains three to five times more nutrients than juice extracted by standard methods; its beneficial enzymes have not been denatured by heat, and because it has been exposed to less oxygen, it will last for a few days when properly refrigerated rather than just for a few hours. Furthermore, this juice is very smooth in consistency; it does not contain any pulp or insoluble fibre. This fibre is left behind in the bags and has been thoroughly wrung of nutrients, though it can still be used in other recipes, such as our Healing Vegetable Broth (page 263). The drawbacks are that it is labour intensive and the machines it relies upon can be prohibitively expensive.

Cold Press

Masticating Juicer

Centrifugal Juicer

Blender

Masticating and Slow Juicers

Masticating and slow juicers are as close to cold presses as you'll get for home use without breaking the bank. They tend to be pricier than centrifugal juicers, but if you're setting out to buy your first juicer, we recommend that you go with one of these; the difference is worth it. They will extract more juice, meaning that you won't have to buy as much produce (believe us, it adds up); they will extract more nutrients from the juice; and they will expose it to less heat and oxygen, making the final product more potent and allowing it to last for up to three days in the fridge without losing its oomph. A masticating juicer is usually horizontally oriented while a slow juicer is upright and looks more like a centrifugal juicer.

Centrifugal Juicers

Inside a centrifugal juicer, sharp metal spins at great speed, chopping and shredding the produce and centrifugally pulling the liquid from the solid through a mesh filter. This extracts less juice than a masticating or slow juicer (especially when it comes to leafy greens and sprouts) and brings more heat (from the friction) and oxygen into the equation. However, these are by far the least expensive juicers on the market—and you're still getting a whole lot of goodness if you're regularly drinking juice extracted this way. The key is to drink it within an hour or two of extracting it, while most of its nutrition is intact.

Blenders

You can do a lot with a blender. In addition to making satisfactory juices, you can make smoothies, nut milks, soups, sauces, desserts or anything that contains liquid. (A food processor is required for mixing when no liquid is involved.) Blenders can get pricey, but the higher price tag is often worth it—a powerful blender will go a long way toward improving the texture of your recipes. If you're juicing using a blender, peel and seed the ingredients, chop them as finely as your blender requires, blend them with a small amount of water until you achieve a smooth mixture and then strain it through a mesh sieve.

The Good

Makes about 2 cups

The name says it all: this one is damned good. In fact, it's better than any other green juice we've ever tried (but we're biased). It contains no sweet fruit, but unlike some of the meaner greens out there, it isn't the least bit swampy. Crisp cucumber and lemon brighten up the leafy greens, and the tiny pinch of salt, while not essential, underscores the natural saltiness of the celery for a bright, savoury finish.

8 cups loosely packed spinach

8 large romaine leaves

½ cucumber, unpeeled, coarsely chopped

1 stalk celery, coarsely chopped

1 lemon, peeled and halved or quartered, white pith intact

Pinch of pink salt or sea salt (optional)

Push the ingredients (except the salt) through your juicer a handful at a time. Running ingredients like lemon in between leafy ingredients like spinach and romaine will help to draw more juice out of the leaves.

Once you have finished running your ingredients through, let the juicer continue to run for a minute or two to extract the maximum amount of juice from the produce left in the machine. Strain the juice using a fine tea sieve to get a nice, smooth texture. Add the pinch of salt (if using). Shake or stir to combine before drinking. Serve chilled.

Store in an airtight container in the fridge for up to 3 days if you're using a masticating juicer or 1 day if you're using a centrifugal juicer or blender.

PRO TIP

For all of our juices, peel the lemons, removing the tough outer rind. Keep as much of the white pith intact as possible if you don't mind the taste, as it is a great source of antioxidants.

East of Eden

Makes about 2 cups

We semi-jokingly call this one our gateway green. If you're trying to convince a first-timer (perhaps yourself) to turn over a new leaf (and then drink it), East of Eden is the place to start. One of our most popular juices, this is a serious garden in a glass with just enough sweetness to lure the naysayers. Kale brings gravitas and a whiff of pungency (a healthy reminder that this juice means business), while romaine cools, lemon brightens, celery deepens and apple seals the deal.

10 large romaine leaves

6 leaves kale

2 stalks celery, coarsely chopped

1½ apples, unpeeled, cored, seeded and coarsely chopped (see pro tip)

1 lemon, peeled and halved or quartered, white pith intact

VARIATION

SOUTH OF EDEN / Spice up your East of Eden and turn up its anti-inflammatory powers with a 2-inch piece of fresh ginger or turmeric (or one of each!).

Push the ingredients through your juicer a handful at a time. Running ingredients like lemon in between leafy ingredients like romaine and kale will help to draw more juice out of the leaves.

Once you have finished running your ingredients through, let the juicer continue to run for a minute or two to extract the maximum amount of juice from the produce left in the machine. Strain the juice using a fine tea sieve to get a nice, smooth texture. Serve chilled.

Store in an airtight container in the fridge for up to 3 days if you're using a masticating juicer or 1 day if you're using a centrifugal juicer or blender.

PRO TIP

Leave the skin on the apples for some added goodness; apple skin is a great source of pectin, a water-soluble fibre that helps with digestion.

Apple seeds contain amygdalin, a cyanide and sugar compound that degrades into hydrogen cyanide (HCN) when metabolized. However, the quantities are small and the seeds' hard, protective shells allow them to largely pass undigested through our digestive systems. So while it's a good idea to remove all of the seeds from apples before juicing them, particularly if you're using a masticating juicer, don't panic; you would have to eat a lot of apple seeds to cause yourself harm.

Gold Rush

Makes about 2 cups

This is a zingy blond with a cult following among the Greenhouse community—especially on those weekend mornings that come too soon. With a strong hit of ginger, this one will kick-start your immune system, making harmful bacteria and viruses tremble in their boots. The silica in cucumber is good for maintaining youthful skin, and an enzyme called bromelain found in pineapple is a natural anti-inflammatory and digestive aid.

2-inch slice pineapple (or 2 cups coarsely chopped), peeled core intact

1 lemon, peeled and halved or quartered, white pith intact

1 cucumber, unpeeled, coarsely chopped

2-inch piece fresh ginger

Push the ingredients through your juicer a handful at a time. Once you have finished running your ingredients through, let the juicer continue to run for a minute or two to extract the maximum amount of juice from the produce left in the machine. Strain the juice using a fine tea sieve to get a nice, smooth texture. Serve chilled.

Store in an airtight container in the fridge for up to 3 days if you're using a masticating juicer or 1 day if you're using a centrifugal juicer or blender.

Wake Up

Makes about 2 cups

On top of being the best breakfast accompaniment on the block (and a serious upgrade from your standard glass of OJ), this tart, spicy juice is immunity boosting and circulation stimulating. We use liquid cayenne (in tincture form, which you can find online or in some health food stores) to help with distribution, but if ground cayenne is all you can find, no problem. Just make sure to stir well so you don't get it all in one super-hot sip!

3 medium oranges

1 ruby red grapefruit

1 lemon

¼ teaspoon ground cayenne pepper or 1 drop liquid cayenne

Slice your oranges, grapefruit and lemon in half. Using a citrus press (hand or mechanized), squeeze their juice into a glass or carafe. If you prefer your citrus juices without pulp, strain the juice using a fine tea sieve.

Add the cayenne, stir well and taste. Continue with another dash or drop if you prefer extreme heat. Shake or stir to combine before drinking. Serve chilled.

Store in an airtight container in the fridge for up to 5 days.

Deep Roots

This juice's flavour comes in layers—earthy, sweet, salty and tangy—that are as well balanced as your yoga instructor in tree pose. It's easy on the palate and extremely hard working; raw beet juice is a rich source of antioxidants, promotes heart health and has been shown to increase stamina during a workout. (It might also turn your pee red. Don't be alarmed.) We love to ground ourselves with this one in the middle of the afternoon when we crave a little something sweet.

1 apple, unpeeled, cored and seeded

½ lemon, peeled, white pith intact

2 medium red beets, leaves and stalks removed, coarsely chopped

3 large carrots, leaves removed, coarsely chopped

2 stalks celery, coarsely chopped

Push the ingredients through your juicer a handful at a time. Let the juicer continue to run for a minute or two to extract the maximum amount of juice. Strain the juice using a fine tea sieve to get a nice, smooth texture. Shake or stir to combine before drinking. Serve chilled.

Store in an airtight container in the fridge for up to 3 days if you're using a masticating juicer or 1 day if you're using a centrifugal juicer or blender.

Rabbit, Run

Makes about 2 cups

Feel an ominous tickle in your throat? Have a runny nose or a throbbing pain behind your temples? This one will patch you up and strengthen your defences. A classic hot-and-sweet combination, its strong dose of ginger, balanced with earthy carrot and soothing apple, boosts immunity, fights inflammation and promotes optimal cell function, all in a day's work.

2 apples, unpeeled, cored, seeded and coarsely chopped

6 medium carrots, leaves removed, coarsely chopped

2-inch piece fresh ginger

Push the ingredients through your juicer a handful at a time. Let the juicer continue to run for a minute or two to extract the maximum amount of juice. Strain the juice using a fine tea sieve to get a nice, smooth texture. Shake or stir to combine before drinking. Serve chilled.

Store in an airtight container in the fridge for up to 3 days if you're using a masticating juicer or 1 day if you're using a centrifugal juicer or blender.

The Giver

Makes about 2 cups

Welcome to the deep end. Earthy, complex and slightly peppery (thanks to the sprouts), The Giver is the most advanced juice you'll find in this book. Let it separate to appreciate the Christmasy effect of the red chard hovering above the dense forest of greens. Serve it very cold. This will become your go-to juice if you happen to be a member of what our former colleague José liked to refer to as "the green juice cognoscenti"—i.e., hard core.

6 leaves collard greens

2 leaves rainbow chard

4 leaves green or red kale

2-inch piece cucumber, unpeeled, coarsely chopped

2 stalks celery, coarsely chopped

Handful of pea shoots (about ¾ cup)

Handful of sunflower sprouts (about ¾ cup)

½ lemon, peeled, white pith intact

2-inch piece fresh ginger

Push the ingredients through your juicer a handful at a time. Running ingredients like lemon in between leafy ingredients like collards, chard and kale will help to draw more juice out of the leaves. Once you have finished running ingredients through, let the juicer continue to run for a minute or two to extract the maximum amount of juice from the produce left in the machine. Strain the juice using a fine tea sieve to get a nice, smooth texture. Shake or stir to combine before drinking. Serve chilled.

Store in an airtight container in the fridge for up to 3 days if you're using a masticating juicer or 1 day if you're using a centrifugal juicer or blender.

The Misfit

Makes about 2 cups

Let's just say you were on fire last night, pulling out dance moves you didn't even know you were capable of. And now it's today. And . . . ow. This juice is there for you. Forget hair of the dog; a few swigs of this stuff and you'll be as good as new. But counteracting overindulgence isn't its only talent; it's also a liver cleanser, a post-workout hydrator, a free radical fighter, a skin purifier . . . and, let's face it, a bit of a weirdo.

4 stalks celery, coarsely chopped

1 small bunch red grapes (2½ cups)

2 limes, peeled, halved,
white pith intact

Run the ingredients through your juicer by the small handful, alternating between celery, grapes and lime to extract the greatest amount of juice possible. Strain the juice using a fine tea sieve to get a nice, smooth texture. Shake or stir to combine before drinking. Serve chilled.

Store in an airtight container in the fridge for up to 3 days if you're using a masticating juicer or 1 day if you're using a centrifugal juicer or blender.

Cabbages and Kings

Makes about 2 cups

The Cruciferous Queen (beautiful, smelly red cabbage) is rich in antioxidants and anti-inflammatory compounds and generously lends her support to digestion and cardiovascular health. The Prickly Prince, meanwhile (HM pineapple), is a well-known benefactor of vitamin C and manganese, among more discreet gifts. Add ginger for immunity (diplomatic and otherwise), zip and sparkle, and you begin to understand why the Walrus gives cabbages and kings so much airtime.

½ small to medium red cabbage, cored (6 large leaves)

1½-inch slice pineapple, peeled, core intact (2½ cups coarsely chopped)

4-inch piece fresh ginger

Run the ingredients through your juicer by the small handful, alternating between folded leaves of cabbage, pineapple and ginger to extract the greatest amount of juice possible. Strain the juice using a fine tea sieve to get a nice, smooth texture. Shake or stir to combine before drinking. Serve chilled.

Store in an airtight container in the fridge for up to 3 days if you're using a masticating juicer or 1 day if you're using a centrifugal juicer or blender.

Oz

Makes about 2 cups

One night during our frigid first winter of existence, a young Australian man named Dean walked into our little house for a working interview. Within a few hours he was an indispensable member of the team. Most of our recipe development is collaborative, but Dean came up with this sweet, warming green juice singlehandedly. We named it for his country of origin—and in reference to his general wizardry.

2 large carrots, leaves removed, scrubbed and coarsely chopped

4 cups loosely packed spinach

½ cucumber, unpeeled, coarsely chopped

½ lemon, peeled, white pith intact

½ jalapeño pepper, stem removed

1-inch slice pineapple, peeled, core intact, coarsely chopped

Push the ingredients through your juicer a handful at a time. Once you have finished running your ingredients through, let the juicer continue to run for a minute or two to extract the maximum amount of juice from the produce left in the machine. Strain the juice using a fine tea sieve to get a nice, smooth texture. Serve chilled.

Store in an airtight container in the fridge for up to 3 days if you're using a masticating juicer or 1 day if you're using a centrifugal juicer or blender.

Harlequin

Makes about 2 cups

Like the mischievous *commedia dell'arte* character, this juice is brighter than you'd expect and vibrating with energy. A subtle-tasting green, it is filled with skin-healthy beta-carotene and will help to restore your electrolytes after a workout. If you're nervous about going green, or if you've got a thirst to quench, try this recipe. It could be the beginning of a beautiful romance.

8 cups loosely packed spinach

8 leaves romaine

1 lime, peeled, halved, white pith intact

1 cup pure young Thai coconut water, preferably unpasteurized and organic (see pro tip)

Push the spinach and romaine through your juicer a handful at a time. Run the lime through in between the leaves. Let the juicer continue to run for a minute or two so it extracts the maximum amount of juice from the produce left in the machine.

Strain the juice using a fine tea sieve to get a nice, smooth texture, then add the coconut water. Shake or stir to combine before drinking. Serve chilled.

Store in an airtight container in the fridge for up to 3 days if you're using a masticating juicer or 1 day if you're using a centrifugal juicer or blender.

PRO TIP

Be aware that even coconuts that are grown organically are usually sprayed before being sent to North America, which undermines their organic status. The purest coconut water we have found in Canada and the United States has been extracted from organic young Thai coconuts and then flash frozen and sent over on dry ice.

We use our own brand of coconut water, which is organic and entirely raw. No matter which brand you try, make sure that there is no added sugar or flavouring.

Boom

Think of this juice as a Bloody Mary that has your best interests at heart. Beets have been shown to increase endurance, so this one is great pre-workout. It's also liver cleansing and blood building, and the beta carotene in the carrots and the lycopene in the tomatoes will help give your skin a healthy glow. Meanwhile, jalapeño heat helps to keep your metabolism revving and the rest of you tingling.

½ lemon, peeled, white pith intact

2 small red beets, leaves and stalks removed, coarsely chopped

3 large carrots, leaves removed, coarsely chopped

3 medium tomatoes (any variety), cored and coarsely chopped

6 stalks cilantro

½ jalapeño pepper, stem removed

Chop the ingredients to fit the opening of your juicer, and run them through a handful at a time. Let the juicer continue to run for a minute or two to extract the maximum amount of juice. Strain the juice using a fine tea sieve to get a nice, smooth texture. Shake or stir to combine before drinking. Serve chilled.

Store in an airtight container in the fridge for up to 3 days if you're using a masticating juicer or 1 day if you're using a centrifugal juicer or blender.

Ophelia

Makes about 2 cups

This is a beautifying juice. The honeydew melon helps to boost collagen, which in turn helps to repair skin and maintain its youthful firmness. Fennel is a digestive aid and good for gut health (as well as being one of the plants that Shakespeare's Ophelia handed out before her death), while rainbow chard contains bone-strengthening minerals. We like to drink this one about an hour before or after a meal to help with digestion.

1-inch slice honeydew melon
(from the middle), seeded
and coarsely chopped

½ lemon, peeled, white pith intact

2 leaves rainbow chard

¼ medium bulb fennel (use bulb
and fronds), coarsely chopped

1 zucchini, unpeeled,
coarsely chopped

Chop the ingredients to fit the opening of your juicer, and run them through a handful at a time. Let the juicer continue to run for a minute or two to extract the maximum amount of juice. Strain the juice using a fine tea sieve to get a nice, smooth texture. Shake or stir to combine before drinking. Serve chilled.

Store in an airtight container in the fridge for up to 3 days if you're using a masticating juicer or 1 day if you're using a centrifugal juicer or blender.

Alpha

You might take one look at these odd ingredients and think, "I'll pass," but we highly recommend you put Alpha to the test. Its provitamin A content, courtesy of the butternut squash and red peppers, is great for your vision, skin and immune system. Throw in some sweet, heart-healthy and vitamin C–boosting oranges and you have one overachieving juice.

2-inch slice butternut squash, seeded, cored, skin on (2 cups coarsely chopped into cubes)

2 small red peppers, seeded (4 cups coarsely chopped)

1½ oranges, peeled and halved or quartered

Push the ingredients through your juicer a handful at a time. Let the juicer continue to run for a minute or two to extract the maximum amount of juice. Strain the juice using a fine tea sieve to get a nice, smooth texture. Shake or stir to combine before drinking. Serve chilled.

Store in an airtight container in the fridge for up to 3 days if you're using a masticating juicer or 1 day if you're using a centrifugal juicer or blender.

TKO

This is the perfect restorative tonic after a big workout. TKO stands for "Technical Knock Out"; kale and turmeric don't pull punches. The former is a source of protein and vitamins A, C and K, and the latter is the most potent natural anti-inflammatory we know of. But the sweet, warming butternut squash and refreshing zucchini and lemon soften the intensity of those two ingredients. If you like heat or if it's a really cold day, we recommend adding some ginger.

¾ lemon, peeled, white pith intact

1-inch slice butternut squash, seeded, cored, skin on (1 cup coarsely chopped into cubes)

1 zucchini, unpeeled, coarsely chopped

2 stalks celery, coarsely chopped

3 leaves kale

1-inch piece fresh turmeric

2-inch piece fresh ginger (optional)

Chop the ingredients to fit the opening of your juicer, and run them through a handful at a time. Let the juicer continue to run for a minute or two to extract the maximum amount of juice. Strain the juice using a fine tea sieve to get a nice, smooth texture. Shake or stir to combine before drinking. Serve chilled.

Store in an airtight container in the fridge for up to 3 days if you're using a masticating juicer or 1 day if you're using a centrifugal juicer or blender.

8½

Makes about 2 cups

Named for the Fellini film, this juice really has only eight ingredients—the half can be inspiration, inflation, or anything that suits your mood. Broccoli leaves, the large outer fronds of the plant that produces broccoli, are still trying to break into the vegetable mainstream; if your local grocer doesn't stock them, try subbing collard greens or chard. Golden beets (sometimes known as yellow beets) have had a bit more time to establish themselves and are somewhat easier to find. They are slightly less sweet than red beets and, crucially, will keep the colour of this juice bright. If you can't find golden beets and are secure enough in your juicing habits to drink something that is slightly brownish, red beets will taste great too.

½ cucumber, unpeeled, coarsely chopped

4 broccoli leaves

4 cups loosely packed spinach

2 small golden beets, scrubbed, leaves and stalks removed

2 stalks celery, coarsely chopped

½ lemon, peeled, white pith intact

8 basil leaves

1-inch piece fresh ginger

Push the ingredients through your juicer a handful at a time. Running ingredients like lemon in between leafy ingredients like broccoli leaves and spinach will help to draw more juice out of the leaves.

Once you have finished running your ingredients through, let the juicer continue to run for a minute or two to extract the maximum amount of juice from the produce left in the machine. Strain the juice using a fine tea sieve to get a nice, smooth texture. Serve chilled.

Store in an airtight container in the fridge for up to 3 days if you're using a masticating juicer or 1 day if you're using a centrifugal juicer or blender.

Juice Cocktails

Because sometimes balance means putting your feet up and/or letting your hair down! Shake these up in a cocktail shaker and serve them over ice in the chilled glass of your choice.

Kale Margarita

1½ ounces tequila
¾ cup East of Eden (page 154)
Juice of ½ lime

Wake Up Negroni

1½ ounces gin
¾ cup Wake Up (page 158)
1 to 2 teaspoons Campari

Dark and Stormy

1½ ounces rum
1½ ounces ginger juice
1½ ounces pure maple syrup
Juice of ½ lime
¼ teaspoon turmeric juice (optional)
Top with sparkling water

Et Tu, Brutus?

1½ ounces vodka
1 cup Boom (page 174)
½ teaspoon horseradish
4 dashes hot sauce
Pinch of freshly ground black pepper
Squeeze of lemon

Smoothies

Rococoa

Makes 1 large smoothie (about 2 cups) or 2 small smoothies (about 1 cup each)

This is one of our two most popular smoothies, and for good reason. We sometimes tell customers that it tastes like chocolate-covered almonds, but that's an oversimplification; most chocolate-covered almonds don't hold a candle to this masterpiece. The name is a play on "raw cacao" (see the description of Choco-Maca-Milk, page 235), on an Arcade Fire song and on the sheer extravagance of this smoothie. It is often mispronounced "ro-coc-*ohhh!*"—again, for good reason.

1 cup Smoothie Milk (page 227) or other non-dairy milk

1 frozen banana, roughly chopped

1 to 2 Medjool dates, pitted

1 tablespoon raw cacao powder

1 teaspoon ground maca (optional)

½ teaspoon coconut oil

1 vanilla bean, sliced lengthwise, seeds scraped out and reserved, or 1 teaspoon pure vanilla extract

1 tablespoon natural almond butter

7 ice cubes

Pour the Smoothie Milk into a blender, ensuring that the blades are submerged. Add the banana, dates, cacao, maca (if using), coconut oil, vanilla seeds or extract and almond butter.

Blend for 30 seconds, or until well combined. If your blender has more than one setting, start on a low speed and slowly build up to a high one to keep everything from jumping toward the lid of your blender and making it harder to clean.

Taste and adjust if necessary, then add the ice cubes and blend on a high speed until smooth. If you can no longer hear the crunch of ice when you switch off the blender and hear the motor winding down, your cubes should be thoroughly pulverized. Pour into a tall glass and serve.

VARIATION

DATELESS / For decreased extravagance, delete the dates and add a big handful of baby spinach or kale.

ROCOCO-LDBREW / Use ½ cup Smoothie Milk and ½ cup Cold-Brew Coffee (page 242) to turn this into the ultimate all-in-one breakfast.

Rio Deal

Makes 1 large smoothie (about 2 cups) or 2 small smoothies (about 1 cup each)

This is our second most popular smoothie. It's feistier than Rococoa (page 189); we compare it to a gingerbread cookie. The ginger and cinnamon lend a good amount of zip, which is nicely balanced by the vanilla. If we're having this one for breakfast or after a workout, we'll sometimes enhance with a tablespoon of hemp seeds or natural almond butter for added protein. A teaspoon of blue-green algae also makes for a healthy, turquoise-hued addition.

1 cup Smoothie Milk (page 227) or other non-dairy milk

1 frozen banana, roughly chopped

1 Medjool date, pitted

½ teaspoon coconut oil

½ teaspoon ground cinnamon

1 vanilla bean, sliced lengthwise, seeds scraped out and reserved, or 1 teaspoon pure vanilla extract

1 heaping teaspoon peeled and grated fresh ginger

7 ice cubes

Pour the Smoothie Milk into a blender, ensuring that the blades are submerged. Add the banana, date, coconut oil, cinnamon, vanilla seeds or extract and ginger.

Blend for 30 seconds, or until well combined. If your blender has more than one setting, start on a low speed and slowly build up to a high one to keep everything from jumping toward the lid of your blender and making it harder to clean.

Taste and adjust if necessary, then add the ice cubes and blend on a high speed until smooth. If you can no longer hear the crunch of ice when you switch off the blender and hear the motor winding down, your cubes should be thoroughly pulverized. Pour into a tall glass and serve.

Picante Green

Makes 1 large smoothie (about 2 cups) or 2 small smoothies (about 1 cup each)

This one is refreshing, spicy and green all over. The combination of bromelain from pineapple, silica from cucumber and beta carotene from spinach makes it an especially great recipe for maintaining healthy skin. Throw in some hydrating coconut water, detoxifying cilantro, tangy lime and metabolism-boosting cayenne, and you've got yourself a great-looking smoothie. Go easy on the cayenne to start and gradually add more. There is a lot of good stuff going on here that you wouldn't want to overpower.

1 cup coconut water

1 cup loosely packed baby spinach

1 cup cubed fresh or
frozen pineapple

½ cup coarsely chopped cucumber

2 teaspoons chopped fresh cilantro

1 teaspoon freshly
squeezed lime juice

Pinch of ground cayenne pepper

3 to 4 ice cubes (optional)

Pour the coconut water into a blender, ensuring that the blades are submerged. Add the spinach, pineapple, cucumber, cilantro, lime juice and cayenne.

Blend for 30 seconds, or until well combined. If your blender has more than one setting, start on a low speed and slowly build up to a high one to keep everything from jumping toward the lid of your blender and making it harder to clean.

Taste and add more cayenne if desired, or other ingredients to taste. If the consistency is too thin, add the ice cubes and a dash more coconut water. Blend on high until smooth. If you can no longer hear the crunch of ice when you switch off the blender and hear the motor winding down, your cubes should be thoroughly pulverized. Pour into a tall glass and serve.

Leo

Makes 1 large smoothie (about 2 cups) or 2 small smoothies (about 1 cup each)

Like both of its maestro namesakes (Da Vinci and the Teenage Mutant Ninja Turtle), this Leo is subtle yet fierce. Matcha brings slow-release energy, ginger brings anti-inflammatory Zen, hemp brings staying power, and kale brings the big guns. Some days we choose to leave out the kiwi and add an extra cup of kale or spinach and a bit more ice for additional nunchucks. If ever a smoothie were capable of inventing the flying machine, it would be this one.

½ cup coconut water

½ cup filtered water

1 cup loosely packed baby kale

1 frozen banana, roughly chopped

1 fresh or frozen kiwi,
peeled and chopped

2 teaspoons peeled and
grated fresh ginger

1 teaspoon hemp seeds

1 teaspoon freshly
squeezed lime juice

½ teaspoon matcha powder

3 to 4 ice cubes (optional)

Pour the coconut water and water into a blender, ensuring that the blades are submerged. Add the kale, banana, kiwi, ginger, hemp seeds, lime juice and matcha.

Blend for 30 seconds, or until well combined. If your blender has more than one setting, start on a low speed and slowly build up to a high one to keep everything from jumping toward the lid of your blender and making it harder to clean.

Taste and adjust flavour if desired by adding more ginger, matcha or lime. If it seems too thin, add the ice cubes and a dash more water. Blend on high until smooth. If you can no longer hear the crunch of ice when you switch off the blender and hear the motor winding down, your cubes should be thoroughly pulverized. Pour into a tall glass and serve.

Berry Eclectic

Makes 1 large smoothie (about 2 cups) or 2 small smoothies (about 1 cup each)

This smoothie is a great snack for when you're in the mood for something sweet, cooling and filled with antioxidants. It's also a perfect way to freeze the summer and drink it all year-round (see pro tip). Chlorella and spirulina are types of blue-green algae that can be found in powdered form at most health food stores. Start with very small amounts and work your way up to the recommended serving size; they can be quite swampy-tasting in large quantities. If you'd prefer not to include algae in your smoothie or don't happen to have any on hand, you can leave it out or add a handful of leafy greens like spinach or kale instead.

1 cup coconut water

1 cup fresh or frozen strawberries

½ cup fresh or frozen blueberries

½ cup fresh or frozen raspberries

1 tablespoon pure maple syrup (optional)

Pinch of chlorella or spirulina powder

Pour the coconut water into a blender, ensuring that the blades are submerged. Add the strawberries, blueberries, raspberries, maple syrup (if using) and chlorella or spirulina.

Blend for 30 seconds, or until well combined. If your blender has more than one setting, start on a low speed and slowly build up to a high one to keep everything from jumping toward the lid of your blender and making it harder to clean.

Taste and adjust flavour or consistency if desired. Blend on high until smooth. Pour into a tall glass and serve.

PRO TIP

If you get a chance, stockpile fresh berries when they are in season and freeze them yourself. We like to make up individual freezer packs with the mixed berries to save time.

Jobim

Makes 1 large smoothie (about 2 cups) or 2 small smoothies (about 1 cup each)

Named for Antônio Carlos Jobim, the Rio-born bossa nova superstar, this smoothie is great for after a workout. Lots of protein, a hit of vitamin C, some fibre and some healthy fats, and off you go.

¾ cup freshly squeezed orange juice

¼ cup Brazil Nut Milk (page 224) or other non-dairy milk

1 frozen banana, roughly chopped

1 teaspoon hemp seeds

1 tablespoon protein powder (we use Raw Power, which is vegan and organic)

7 ice cubes

Pour the orange juice and Brazil Nut Milk into a blender, ensuring that the blades are submerged. Add the banana, hemp seeds and protein powder.

Blend for 30 seconds, or until well combined. If your blender has more than one setting, start on a low speed and slowly build up to a high one to keep everything from jumping toward the lid of your blender and making it harder to clean.

Taste and adjust flavour or consistency if desired. Add ice cubes and blend on high until smooth. If you can no longer hear the crunch of ice when you switch off the blender and hear the motor winding down, your cubes should be thoroughly pulverized. Pour into a tall glass and serve.

Firefly

Makes 1 large smoothie (about 2 cups) or 2 small smoothies (about 1 cup each)

Named for Noël Coward's house in the hills above Oracabessa, Jamaica, where he and Ian Fleming used to hang out, Firefly tastes like the island that inspired it. Turmeric is a strong natural inflammation fighter, and camu camu berry, which you can find powdered at health food stores or online, is one of the most concentrated natural sources of vitamin C. If you can't find camu camu, you can leave it out or replace it with a handful of your choice of berries.

1¼ cups Smoothie Milk (page 227) or other non-dairy milk

½ frozen banana, coarsely chopped

1½ cups cubed fresh or frozen mango

1 Medjool date, pitted

1 teaspoon peeled and grated fresh turmeric

2 teaspoons freshly squeezed lemon juice

¼ teaspoon camu camu berry powder

3 to 4 ice cubes (optional)

Pour the Smoothie Milk into a blender, ensuring that the blades are submerged. Add the banana, mango, date, turmeric, lemon juice and camu camu berry powder.

Blend for 30 seconds, or until well combined. If your blender has more than one setting, start on a low speed and slowly build up to a high one to keep everything from jumping toward the lid of your blender and making it harder to clean.

Check flavour and consistency, add the ice cubes if desired and blend on high until smooth. If you can no longer hear the crunch of ice when you switch off the blender and hear the motor winding down, your cubes should be thoroughly pulverized. Pour into a tall glass and serve.

Sweet Potato Chai

Makes 1 large smoothie (about 2 cups) or 2 small smoothies (about 1 cup each)

The pumpkin spice craze, immoderate and far removed from actual pumpkins as it may be, is, in our opinion, entirely justified. What could be more comforting when the leaves start to change than a warm sweater and something sweet to sip on that tastes of cinnamon, ginger and cloves? In this variation, we've gone from pumpkin to sweet potato to make the roasting part a little easier, and from pie to chai.

1 large sweet potato

½ cup Smoothie Milk (page 227) or other non-dairy milk

½ cup Chai Concentrate (page 243)

1½ Medjool dates, pitted

1 tablespoon pumpkin seeds, plus extra for topping

Pinch of ground cinnamon, plus extra for topping

Pinch of ground ginger, nutmeg, cloves and/or allspice (optional)

½ teaspoon pure vanilla extract (optional)

7 ice cubes

Preheat the oven to 350°F.

Scrub the sweet potato and use a fork to poke a number of holes in its skin, piercing the flesh. This will allow steam to escape while it is roasting. Place the sweet potato directly on the centre oven rack, with a piece of aluminum foil positioned beneath to catch drops of sticky goodness. Bake for 1 hour, or until it is very soft and easily pierced when prodded with a fork. Remove from oven. Let the sweet potato cool, then remove the skin. It should come off fairly easily once it has cooled.

Combine the Smoothie Milk, Chai Concentrate, sweet potato, dates, pumpkin seeds and cinnamon in a blender, and blend on high speed for 30 seconds, or until smooth.

Taste the mixture and adjust sweetness, spiciness, seediness or liquidness if necessary. Depending on the strength of spice you're after, you may wish to add another half date, a pinch of extra ground cinnamon, ginger, nutmeg, cloves and/or allspice (if using), and ½ teaspoon vanilla (if using).

Add the ice cubes and blend on high until ice is completely crushed. Pour into a tall glass, top with pumpkin seeds and a sprinkle of cinnamon and serve.

VARIATION

PUMPKIN SPICE / If you're a traditionalist and would prefer to stick to the pie trail, substitute the mashed roasted sweet potato with an equivalent amount of roasted or canned pumpkin, use a full cup of nut milk instead of the chai concentrate and add ½ to 1 teaspoon pre-blended pumpkin pie spice (or a mix of the spices above), to taste.

Radio

Makes 1 large smoothie (about 2 cups) or 2 small smoothies (about 1 cup each)

Have you ever heard someone joke that they have a "face for radio"? Well, that's definitely true of this smoothie. The combination of raw spinach and raw cacao—while nutritionally very attractive—will hurt this guy's chances on the smoothie beauty pageant circuit. But it's worth it: the richly flavoured cacao provides fibre and antioxidants with no sugar, and it completely overpowers the taste of the energizing, vitamin-rich mountain of spinach. Ground flax seed and natural peanut butter add body, more fibre, protein, and healthy fats, while the frozen banana sweetens and the ginger provides some anti-inflammatory zip.

¾ cup Smoothie Milk (page 227) or other non-dairy milk

1 frozen banana, roughly chopped

2 cups loosely packed baby spinach

1 tablespoon ground or whole flax seeds

2 teaspoons raw cacao powder

1 tablespoon natural peanut butter

1 to 2 teaspoons juiced ginger, or peeled and grated ginger

7 ice cubes

Whole flax seeds, raw cacao nibs and unsweetened coconut flakes, for garnish

Pour the Smoothie Milk into a blender, ensuring that the blades are submerged. Add the banana, spinach, flax, cacao powder, peanut butter and ginger.

Blend for 30 seconds, or until well combined. If your blender has more than one setting, start on a low speed and slowly build up to a high one to keep everything from jumping toward the lid of your blender and making it harder to clean.

Taste and adjust if necessary, then add the ice cubes and blend on a high speed until smooth. If you can no longer hear the crunch of ice when you switch off the blender and hear the motor winding down, your cubes should be thoroughly pulverized. Pour into a tall glass and serve, topped with flax seeds, cacao nibs and coconut.

Black Seed

Makes 1 large smoothie (about 2 cups) or 2 small smoothies (about 1 cup each)

This is an attempt to recreate (in smoothie form) the black sesame ice cream at our favourite Japanese restaurant. You can find black tahini in a health food store or online. It is a deeper, nuttier and more distinctive version of its beige counterpart, and in concert with nut milk, it achieves something very similar to the creamy original. We arguably got a bit carried away with the addition of mint and cacao nibs; we love the mint-chocolate-chip effect they bring, which somehow works well with the black sesame, but we won't be offended if you leave them out.

1 cup Smoothie Milk (page 227) or other non-dairy milk

1 frozen banana, roughly chopped

2 teaspoons black tahini

1 Medjool date, pitted

½ teaspoon ground cinnamon

1 teaspoon pure vanilla extract

1 teaspoon raw cacao nibs, plus extra for garnish

4 drops peppermint extract or 1 heaping tablespoon chopped fresh mint

7 ice cubes

Pour the Smoothie Milk into a blender, ensuring that the blades are submerged. Add the banana, black tahini, date, cinnamon, vanilla, cacao nibs and mint.

Blend for 30 seconds, or until well combined. If your blender has more than one setting, start on a low speed and slowly build up to a high one to keep everything from jumping toward the lid of your blender and making it harder to clean.

Taste and adjust if necessary, then add the ice cubes and blend on a high speed until smooth. If you can no longer hear the crunch of ice when you switch off the blender and hear the motor winding down, your cubes should be thoroughly pulverized. Pour into a tall glass and serve topped with cacao nibs.

Wild Oats

Makes 1 large smoothie (about 2 cups) or 2 small smoothies (about 1 cup each)

For those mornings when you're craving a fully loaded bowl of porridge but you don't have quite enough time to pull it off, this smoothie is just the ticket. If you're organized, soak your oats overnight at room temperature—just put them in a glass and cover them with filtered water and a plate, then strain and rinse them in the morning—but to be honest, we tend to make this one on a whim, and tossing the oats in dry has worked for us thus far. The almond butter, oats and hemp seeds keep you full for hours, while the cinnamon helps to regulate blood sugar, the spinach charges your batteries, and the psyllium seed husks (if you choose to use it; it's just as good without, albeit not quite as thick) helps with digestion. We don't like our oats very sweet, so this smoothie isn't either; you can add a pitted date or a teaspoon of pure maple syrup if you like an extra bit of sweetness.

1 cup Smoothie Milk (page 227) or other non-dairy milk

¾ frozen banana, roughly chopped

1 cup loosely packed baby spinach

⅓ cup gluten-free rolled oats, soaked overnight (see headnote)

1 tablespoon natural almond butter

1 tablespoon hemp seeds, plus extra for garnish

2 teaspoons psyllium seed husks (optional)

1 teaspoon pure vanilla extract

1 teaspoon ground cinnamon

7 ice cubes

Blueberries, chia seeds, crushed almonds and toasted unsweetened coconut flakes, for garnish

Pour the Smoothie Milk into a blender, ensuring that the blades are submerged. Add the banana, spinach, oats, almond butter, hemp seeds, psyllium seed husks (if using), vanilla and cinnamon.

Blend for 30 seconds, or until well combined. If your blender has more than one setting, start on a low speed and slowly build up to a high one to keep everything from jumping toward the lid of your blender and making it harder to clean.

Taste and adjust if necessary, then add the ice cubes and blend on high until smooth. If you can no longer hear the crunch of ice when you switch off the blender and hear the motor winding down, your cubes should be thoroughly pulverized. Pour into a tall glass and serve topped with hemp seeds, or garnish of your choice.

Pistachio, Cardamom and Rose Water Lassi

Makes about 1 cup

Lassi is a sweet or savoury Indian drink traditionally made from yogurt or buttermilk. For a dairy-free version, use coconut yogurt (available in most health food stores or well-stocked grocery stores) or our Cashew "Yogurt" (page 39). In India, lassi is often served alongside a spicy meal as a cooling agent. This lassi tastes especially good with the Very Veggie Curry with Exploded Yellow Lentils (page 87) or the Lentils and Brown Rice with Rainbow Chard, Roasted Carrots and Tahini (page 79).

2 pods cardamom

⅔ cup non-dairy yogurt

5 raw pistachios, shelled, plus extra, shelled and crushed, for garnish

1 tablespoon pure maple syrup (see pro tip)

¼ teaspoon rose water

¼ teaspoon pure vanilla extract

2 tablespoons filtered water, or more depending on your yogurt's thickness (optional)

6 ice cubes

Remove the cardamom seeds from their pods by smashing the pods with the back of a knife and scraping out the seeds. In a blender, combine the yogurt, shelled pistachios, cardamom seeds, maple syrup, rose water and vanilla.

Blend for 30 seconds, or until well combined. If your blender has more than one setting, start on a low speed and slowly build up to the highest speed.

Taste and adjust flavour and/or add water if necessary (depending on the thickness of your yogurt). Add the ice cubes and blend on a high speed until smooth. If you can no longer hear the crunch of ice when you switch off the blender and hear the motor winding down, your cubes should be thoroughly pulverized. Pour into a tall glass and serve topped with crushed pistachios.

PRO TIP

If you're serving this lassi as a dessert or special treat, add extra maple syrup to taste.

Mint and Black Pepper Savoury Lassi

Makes about 1 cup

We like to make a big pitcher of this savoury lassi for the dinner table if we're having friends over for a spicy meal. Depending on the size of your blender, you can double or quadruple the recipe, or do it in batches. You can make it up to a few hours ahead of time and keep it in the fridge. We also love this one as a filling afternoon snack.

⅔ cup non-dairy yogurt

2 tablespoons loosely packed dried mint

1 tablespoon freshly squeezed lemon juice

Pinch of sea salt

Pinch of freshly ground black pepper

2 tablespoons filtered water, or more depending on your yogurt's thickness (optional)

6 ice cubes

In a blender, combine yogurt, mint, lemon juice, salt and pepper.

Blend for 30 seconds, or until well combined. If your blender has more than one setting, start on a low speed and slowly build up to the highest speed.

Taste and adjust flavour and/or add water if necessary (depending on the thickness of your yogurt). Add the ice cubes and blend on a high speed until smooth. If you can no longer hear the crunch of ice when you switch off the blender and hear the motor winding down, your cubes should be thoroughly pulverized. Pour into a tall glass and serve.

Nut Milks

Soaking Nuts

Most nuts and seeds should be soaked before you use them in nut milks. Also known as activating, soaking makes nuts and seeds more digestible and allows you to better absorb their nutrients. It also helps you squeeze more milk out of every batch.

Begin by sorting through your raw, unsalted nuts or seeds and discarding any rotten scoundrels. Then rinse them and place them in a container with enough filtered water to cover them. Lay a tea towel or piece of cloth over the container and leave them to soak for between two and eight hours. Here are our recommended soaking times for the nuts and seeds used in this section:

Almonds	Eight hours or overnight
Cashews	Two to four hours
Brazil nuts	Three hours
Pumpkin seeds	Eight hours or overnight
Sunflower seeds	Eight hours or overnight
Hemp seeds	No need to soak

If you're soaking overnight and it is warm in your kitchen, we recommend leaving your submerged nuts or seeds in the fridge to keep them from going rancid.

In a pinch, soaking your nuts or seeds in hot water for 10 to 20 minutes will do the trick, but the catch is that by exposing them to high temperatures, you'll lose some of their nutritional oomph.

Once the nuts and seeds have been satisfactorily soaked (more bad guys may have floated to the top; discard these), strain and rinse them thoroughly, discarding the water.

While the nut milks in this section will generally keep for two to three days in an airtight container in the fridge, please don't hold us to that; nut and seed milks can be unpredictable. When nut or seed milk goes bad, it gives off a funky, sour smell and sometimes thickens or becomes slightly bubbly. If any of these things are happening, your milk is past the point of no return.

Almond Milk

Makes about 2 cups

One of our first claims to fame at Greenhouse was this take on handmade almond milk. Decadent and substantial, it feels and tastes far more like a milkshake than like any store-bought almond milk that we've ever experienced. This is partially because we use a higher ratio of nuts to water than is usually recommended—though the rich coconut oil, soft Medjool dates, vanilla bean and pinch of salt help too. We like to use this milk as a base for Choco-Maca-Milk (page 235), Green Milk (page 231) and Pink Milk (page 228).

2 cups raw almonds, soaked (see page 216)

4 Medjool dates, pitted and chopped

1 vanilla bean, sliced lengthwise, seeds scraped out and reserved, or 1 teaspoon pure vanilla extract

1 tablespoon coconut oil (optional)

Pinch of sea salt (optional)

3 cups filtered water, divided

In a blender, combine the almonds, dates, vanilla seeds or extract, coconut oil and salt (if using) and 1 cup water. Blend on low until combined. Add the remaining 2 cups water to the blender and blend for 1 minute, or until smooth.

To strain the milk, place a nut milk bag or a large sieve lined with two layers of cheesecloth over a large bowl. If using cheesecloth, make sure that there is enough cloth hanging over the edges of the sieve to allow you to gather the ends and create a pouch. Pour half of the mixture into the bag or the centre of the cloth, gather the cloth (if using) into a pouch, and squeeze the nut milk through the bag or through the cloth and sieve into the bowl. Once you've squeezed out all of the liquid from the first half of the mixture, empty the fibre into another container and strain the remaining mixture. Use the leftover fibre in the Double Cacao Protein Bites (page 123), Apple Pecan Squares with Caramel Sauce (page 136) or Spiced Grain-Free Granola with Brazil Nut Fibre (page 45).

Serve the milk chilled. Seal in an airtight container and keep in the fridge for up to 3 days.

Cashew Milk

Makes about 3 cups

Cashews are actually the seed of the cashew apple, a fruit that grows on trees in Brazil. Naturally creamy, cashews are frequently used as a dairy substitute. Their softness means that they don't need to be soaked for very long, and because of their richness, we use a lower nut-to-water ratio than we would in our Almond Milk (page 219) and omit the coconut oil. This milk is a great base for Matcha Ginger Milk (page 236).

2 cups raw cashews, soaked (see page 216)

2 to 3 Medjool dates, pitted and chopped

1 vanilla bean, sliced lengthwise, seeds scraped out and reserved, or 1 teaspoon pure vanilla extract

Pinch of sea salt (optional)

4 cups filtered water, divided

In a blender, combine the cashews, dates, vanilla seeds or extract, salt (if using) and 2 cups water. Blend on low until combined. Add the remaining 2 cups water to the blender and blend for 1 minute, or until smooth.

To strain the milk, place a nut milk bag or a large sieve lined with two layers of cheesecloth over a large bowl. If using cheesecloth, make sure that there is enough cloth hanging over the edges of the sieve to allow you to gather the ends and create a pouch. Pour half of the mixture into the bag or the centre of the cloth, gather the cloth (if using) into a pouch, and squeeze the nut milk through the bag or through the cloth and sieve into the bowl. Once you've squeezed out all of the liquid from the first half of the mixture, empty the fibre into another container and strain the remaining mixture. Use the leftover fibre in the Double Cacao Protein Bites (page 123), Apple Pecan Squares with Caramel Sauce (page 136) or Spiced Grain-Free Granola with Brazil Nut Fibre (page 45).

Serve the milk chilled. Seal in an airtight container and keep in the fridge for up to 3 days.

Combo Nut and Seed Milk

Makes about 2 cups

This milk is a bit seedy, both in taste and in appearance (the sunflower seeds give it a greyish tinge), but frankly that's what we like about it. Unique, multi-functional and rich in protein and healthy fats, this is a great alternative to classic nut milks. Feel free to double one kind of seed and eliminate another as you see fit (based on sensitivity, preference or what you have in your pantry). This makes a great base for Harvest Milk (page 232).

½ cup raw cashews, soaked
(see page 216)

¼ cup raw sunflower seeds, soaked

¼ cup raw pumpkin seeds, soaked

¼ cup hemp seeds

2 Medjool dates, pitted
and chopped

¼ vanilla bean, sliced lengthwise,
seeds scraped out and reserved,
or ¼ teaspoon pure vanilla extract

3 cups filtered water, divided

In a blender, combine the cashews, sunflower seeds, pumpkin seeds, hemp seeds, dates, vanilla seeds or extract and 1 cup water. Blend on low until combined. Add the remaining 2 cups water to the blender and blend for 1 minute, or until smooth.

To strain the milk, place a nut milk bag or a large sieve lined with two layers of cheesecloth over a large bowl. If using cheesecloth, make sure that there is enough cloth hanging over the edges of the sieve to allow you to gather the ends and create a pouch. Pour half of the mixture into the bag or the centre of the cloth, gather the cloth (if using) into a pouch, and squeeze the nut milk through the bag or through the cloth and sieve into the bowl. Once you've squeezed out all of the liquid from the first half of the mixture, empty the fibre into another container and strain the remaining mixture. (Use the leftover fibre in a smoothie or rehydrated in a bowl of oatmeal.)

Serve the milk chilled. Seal in an airtight container and keep in the fridge for up to 3 days.

Brazil Nut Milk

Makes about 3 cups

Brazil nuts, like cashews, are seeds masquerading as nuts. They are rich in selenium, a mineral that supports immunity. They also provide vitamin E, which helps to maintain healthy skin, and thiamine, a B-complex vitamin that helps with efficient carbohydrate metabolism and promotes a healthy brain and memory.

3 cups raw Brazil nuts, soaked (see page 216)

5 Medjool dates, pitted and chopped

1 vanilla bean, sliced lengthwise, seeds scraped out and reserved, or 1 teaspoon pure vanilla extract

Pinch of sea salt (optional)

4 cups filtered water, divided

In a blender, combine the Brazil nuts, dates, vanilla seeds or extract, salt (if using) and 2 cups water. Blend on low until combined. Add the remaining 2 cups water to the blender and blend for 1 minute, or until smooth.

To strain the milk, place a nut milk bag or a large sieve lined with two layers of cheesecloth over a large bowl. If using cheesecloth, make sure that there is enough cloth hanging over the edges of the sieve to allow you to gather the ends and create a pouch. Pour half of the mixture into the bag or the centre of the cloth, gather the cloth (if using) into a pouch, and squeeze the nut milk through the bag or through the cloth and sieve into the bowl. Once you've squeezed out all of the liquid from the first half of the mixture, empty the fibre into another container and strain the remaining mixture. Use the leftover fibre in the Double Cacao Protein Bites (page 123), Apple Pecan Squares with Caramel Sauce (page 136) or Spiced Grain-Free Granola with Brazil Nut Fibre (page 45).

Serve the milk chilled. Seal in an airtight container and keep in the fridge for up to 3 days.

PRO TIP

The healthy oils in Brazil nuts will solidify at cold temperatures, forming a hard layer on top of the milk. This is perfectly natural. A few minutes before serving, simply let it sit at room temperature until the oils have softened, then shake or stir to dissolve them. They can also be scooped off, but this would be a shame; these high-quality fats are wonderful for healthy hair, skin and nails, and they help to keep you full for hours at a stretch.

Smoothie Milk

Makes about 3 cups

This is a Greenhouse staple. We use it in our daily smoothies (hence the name), in our breakfast bowls or in any recipe calling for milk. For neutral-tasting milk, we use almonds. For a rich, slightly cinnamony milk that's excellent for giving an extra layer of depth to smoothies, we use Brazil nuts. We include the vanilla if we are making this milk for use in sweet recipes or smoothies and leave it out when using the milk in a savoury recipe like the Spiralized Zucchini Mac and Cheese with Oat Crumb Crust (page 83).

1 cup raw almonds or Brazil nuts, soaked (see page 216)

4 cups filtered water, divided

1 vanilla bean, sliced lengthwise, seeds scraped out and reserved, or 1 teaspoon pure vanilla extract (omit for savoury recipes)

In a blender, combine the almonds or Brazil nuts with 2 cups water and vanilla seeds or extract, if you're using it. Blend on low until well mixed. Add the remaining 2 cups water and blend on high for 1 minute, or until smooth.

To strain the milk, place a nut milk bag or a large sieve lined with two layers of cheesecloth over a large bowl. If using cheesecloth, make sure that there is enough cloth hanging over the edges of the sieve to allow you to gather the ends and create a pouch. Pour half of the mixture into the bag or the centre of the cloth, gather the cloth (if using) into a pouch, and squeeze the nut milk through the bag or through the cloth and sieve into the bowl. Once you've squeezed out all of the liquid from the first half of the mixture, empty the fibre into another container and strain the remaining mixture. Use the leftover fibre in the Double Cacao Protein Bites (page 123), Apple Pecan Squares with Caramel Sauce (page 136) or Spiced Grain-Free Granola with Brazil Nut Fibre (page 45).

Serve the milk chilled. Seal in an airtight container and keep in the fridge for up to 3 days.

Pink Milk

Makes about 1½ cups

In the absence of an aversion to beets, this is the best possible recipe for persuading a suspicious person (big or small) to try vegetable juice. It comes out a vibrant vermilion and tastes like dessert, especially if you add that extra dash of maple syrup (not necessary, but pleasing to a sweet tooth). Serve in fancy teacups for an unforgettable after-school (or after-anything) snack.

3 medium red beets, leaves and stems removed (about ½ cup juiced)

1 cup Almond Milk (page 219)

1 teaspoon pure maple syrup (optional)

Scrub, trim and chop the beets, then run them through your juicer into a measuring cup. This should yield roughly ½ cup beet juice. If your yield falls short, juice more beets or adjust the Almond Milk accordingly.

In a large bowl, whisk the beet juice into the Almond Milk, ensuring that they are well combined. The mixture should be quite sweet, thanks to the dates in the Almond Milk and the natural sweetness of the beets. However, if you (or your target market) prefer it even sweeter, add a teaspoon of pure maple syrup and whisk again.

Refrigerate in an airtight container (such as a mason jar), and serve as soon as it has chilled to your preferred temperature. Drink within a few hours for best results.

Green Milk

Makes about 1½ cups

If it weren't for the colour, you would never believe that this drink was a vehicle for vegetables. The raw spinach is amazingly subtle. Try a blind taste test on a willing candidate and see if he or she can guess. The vivid green colour gives it away, however, and makes you feel pretty darned good about yourself for drinking this delicious concoction first thing in the morning. Trying to make a glass last more than 12 seconds is the only hard part.

8 cups loosely packed spinach, or roughly 2 bunches (about ½ cup juiced)

1 cup Almond Milk (page 219)

1 tablespoon pure maple syrup (optional)

Wash the spinach carefully. Run it through your juicer a small handful at a time; there is no need to separate the leaves from the stems. Use a measuring cup to capture the juice. This should yield roughly ½ cup dark green spinach juice. If your yield falls short, juice more spinach or adjust the Almond Milk accordingly.

In a large bowl, whisk the spinach juice into the Almond Milk, ensuring that they are well combined. Taste the mixture and add maple syrup if desired.

Refrigerate in an airtight container (such as a mason jar), and serve as soon as it has chilled to your preferred temperature. Drink within a few hours for best results.

PRO TIP

Green Milk is extremely sensitive to time and oxidation. While the Almond Milk and spinach get along famously for the first few hours of their lives together, they should not be left to linger in each other's company for longer than that. Otherwise, like siblings trapped in the backseat of a car, less refined sides of their respective personalities will begin to show through.

Harvest Milk

Makes about 1½ cups

Served cold or warm, this is the taste of fall in a glass. Butternut squash is an excellent source of beta carotene, which converts to provitamin A in the body, supporting healthy skin, vision and immunity. If you are looking for more of a pumpkin spice experience, replace the cardamom with pumpkin pie spice (available in many grocery stores) or with a small pinch each of ground cloves, nutmeg and allspice. Because we are dealing with such a small volume here, go very easy on all of the spices to begin with, and add as necessary.

1-inch slice butternut squash, skin intact, coarsely chopped (about ¼ cup juiced)

1 medium sweet potato, skin intact, coarsely chopped (about ¾ cup juiced)

1½-inch piece fresh ginger, coarsely chopped (about 1 tablespoons juiced)

¾ cup Combo Nut and Seed Milk (page 223) or Almond Milk (page 219)

¼ teaspoon ground cinnamon

⅛ teaspoon ground cardamom

½ teaspoon pure vanilla extract

Run the butternut squash, sweet potato and ginger through the juicer, using a measuring cup to capture the juice. This should yield roughly ¼ cup juiced butternut squash, ¾ cup juiced sweet potato, and 3 teaspoons juiced ginger. If any of your yields fall short, juice a bit more or adjust ratios accordingly.

In a large bowl, whisk together the Combo Nut and Seed Milk or Almond Milk, butternut squash juice, sweet potato juice, ginger juice, cinnamon, cardamom and vanilla. Adjust spices to taste.

Refrigerate in an airtight container (such as a mason jar), and serve as soon as it has chilled to your preferred temperature. Drink within a few hours for best results.

PRO TIP

To serve warm, slowly heat up your Harvest Milk in a heavy-bottomed pot or pan. Just be careful not to let it reach a boil! Serve in a mug with a dusting of cinnamon.

Some find that juiced sweet potato, while deliciously sweet, has a slightly starchy or chalky texture. Instead of sweet potato, use 1 cup butternut squash juice to make a brighter drink without the starchiness. It will be less sweet, so add 1 teaspoon maple syrup if desired.

Choco-Maca-Milk

Makes about 2 cups

Picture the best chocolate milk you've ever had, but without dairy or refined sugar. Cacao (pronounced ka-kow) is a raw powder made by cold pressing unroasted cacao beans to remove the cacao butter, or the fat that gives chocolate its creamy texture. Cocoa powder is similar, only it's made from roasted cocoa beans so the powder is not raw and thus does not contain the same beneficial enzymes. Both are good sources of antioxidants and fibre. You can use either in this recipe. Maca root, grown in the mountains of Peru, offers B vitamins, minerals and enzymes and lends a nutty, decadent quality to this irresistible concoction.

2 cups Almond Milk (page 219) or other nut or seed milk (see pro tip)

4 heaping teaspoons raw cacao or unsweetened cocoa powder

1½ heaping teaspoons ground maca (see pro tip)

In a large bowl, whisk together the Almond Milk, cacao and maca. Serve chilled. Seal in an airtight container and keep in the fridge for up to 3 days.

PRO TIP

Make your base nut milk with an extra Medjool date to make this treat even more decadent.

This recipe is just as delicious without the maca. If you are pregnant or breastfeeding, or if you are making this recipe for a child, consider omitting the maca. Do omit the maca if you have a thyroid condition.

VARIATION

CHOCO-MINT MILK / For a mint chocolate variation, omit the maca and add a drop or two of peppermint extract. (Taste after one drop and add another if desired.)

Matcha Ginger Milk

Makes about 1 cup

In what admittedly may be a somewhat heavy-handed use of this delightfully delicate powdered tea, we love whisking a big spoonful of matcha into our Cashew Milk (page 220) with a shot of freshly pressed ginger (not necessary, but quite warming and lovely). Served hot or cold, this is an energizing, anti-inflammatory late-morning or early afternoon indulgence.

1½-inch piece fresh ginger (about 3 teaspoons juiced; see pro tip)

1 teaspoon matcha powder

1 cup Cashew Milk (page 220) or other nut or seed milk

½ teaspoon pure maple syrup, to taste

Run the ginger through your juicer.

In a bowl, whisk the matcha powder into the Cashew Milk using a regular whisk or a special wooden matcha whisk, if you have one. Taste it. Add the ginger juice a bit at a time, until it has reached a level of gingeriness that pleases your palate (everyone's ginger threshold is different; ours is almost infinite). Add the maple syrup if desired, and whisk again to combine.

This is wonderful served over ice in the spring or summer, or slowly warmed up in a heavy-bottomed pot or pan in the fall or winter. Just be careful not to let it reach a boil.

Seal in an airtight container and keep in the fridge for 2 to 3 days.

PRO TIP

While you have your juicer out, you might as well juice a whole knob of ginger. You can drink it alone as a great anti-inflammatory, immunity-boosting shot. It tastes like fire and warms your insides in the most incredible way. It's the perfect thing to take right before a flight; it helps to keep your back and neck from seizing up and guards against plane germs and nausea. We also love to add freshly pressed ginger to a cup of hot water for the perfect after-dinner digestive aid. It will keep for 2 to 3 days sealed in the fridge.

Coconut Milk

Makes about 2 cups

While coconut meat, the white lining found just inside the shell of the coconut, is high in saturated fat, it is mostly of a type known as lauric acid—a beneficial type of saturated fat that has been shown to boost levels of "good" cholesterol, or HDL. Coconut water, meanwhile, is rich in potassium and essential minerals. We like to blend the juicy flesh and unpasteurized, additive-free water from young Thai coconuts to make our own Coconut Milk, which we drink on its own as a post-workout snack, add to smoothies for a rich, satiating boost or whip into cream to top decadent desserts.

½ cup coarsely chopped young Thai coconut meat

2 cups pure young Thai coconut water, preferably unpasteurized and organic

In a blender, combine the coconut meat and coconut water and blend on low for 1 minute.

To strain the milk, place a nut milk bag or a large sieve lined with two layers of cheesecloth over a large bowl. If using cheesecloth, make sure that there is enough cloth hanging over the edges of the sieve to allow you to gather the ends and create a pouch. Pour half of the mixture into the bag or the centre of the cloth, gather the cloth (if using) into a pouch, and squeeze the nut milk through the bag or through the cloth and sieve into the bowl. Once you've squeezed out all of the liquid from the first half of the mixture, empty the fibre into another container and strain the remaining mixture. (Use the leftover fibre in a smoothie or rehydrated in a bowl of oatmeal.)

Serve the milk chilled. Store in an airtight container in the fridge for up to 3 days.

PRO TIP

This Coconut Milk makes a great frozen treat. Pour the blended milk into an ice-pop mould (or the freezer-safe vessel of your choice) with some kiwi and strawberry slices or with a handful of blueberries and raspberries, plus a wooden stick. Freeze for a few hours until solid, and voila!

Piloto

Makes 1 cup

This is a drink we developed using cold-brew coffee from our friends at Pilot Coffee Roasters in Toronto and our rich, nutty Brazil Nut Milk (page 224). Cold-brew coffee is less acidic than hot-brewed coffee, making it easier on the stomach. It's also the tastiest way to appreciate chilled or iced coffee, in our opinion, as you don't have to contend with the usual scourges of wateriness or bitterness. You can either use store-bought unsweetened cold brew or make your own Cold-Brew Coffee (page 242). Just be aware that cold brew has more caffeine than espresso; remember to fasten your seatbelt.

½ cup Cold-Brew Coffee (page 242) or store-bought

½ cup Brazil Nut Milk (page 224) or other non-dairy milk

Cinnamon, for garnish

Combine the coffee and nut milk and serve chilled or over ice with a sprinkle of cinnamon. Store in an airtight container in the fridge for up to 3 days.

Cold-Brew Coffee

Makes about 4 cups

Making your own cold-brew coffee is simple, but you'll need to plan ahead. Instead of relying on heat to extract coffee from the beans, you'll be using time. To make 4 cups of strong cold brew, you will need about 16 hours of brewing time.

¾ cup coffee beans

4 cups cold filtered water

YOU WILL ALSO NEED

1 large sealable jar or a French press

Fine-mesh kitchen sieve

1 large bowl

Cheesecloth or a nut milk bag

Grind your coffee beans very coarsely. You want them to be roughly the consistency of breadcrumbs.

In a jar or French press, combine the ground coffee and water, stirring to ensure that all of the grounds get saturated. Seal with a lid (or with the top of the French press turned to the side to keep oxygen out, but don't press down), and leave it to steep in the fridge for 12 to 24 hours. We find 16 hours to be the sweet spot.

When the brew has finished steeping, place the sieve over a large bowl and strain the coffee through it (or plunge the French press). Discard the grounds. Rinse the original vessel and strain the brew again into it (or into the jar you want your cold brew to live in), this time through two layers of cheesecloth or a nut milk bag. Discard the second round of grounds. If there is still some silt in your coffee, strain again, and try grinding more coarsely next time. The resulting cold-brew coffee lasts in the fridge for about 3 to 4 days.

Chai Concentrate

Everyone's idea of the perfect spice combination is slightly different. We like this version. You may also wish to add in some nutmeg or allspice. If you can find whole cloves, cardamom pods or seeds and cinnamon sticks (any well-stocked grocery store or spice shop should have them), go for it—the aromatic and visceral satisfaction of giving them a quick smash with a mortar and pestle is well worth it.

1-inch piece fresh ginger, coarsely chopped (about 1 tablespoon)

1 teaspoon whole cloves or ½ teaspoon ground cloves

1 stick cinnamon or 1 teaspoon ground cinnamon

7 pods cardamom or ½ teaspoon ground cardamom

1 teaspoon freshly ground black pepper

1 tablespoon or 2 emptied bags of strong black tea, such as Assam or Lipton Yellow Label

2 cups filtered water

Combine the ginger, cloves, cinnamon and cardamom in a mortar or heavy-bottomed pot, and give them a good smash with a pestle or with the back of a spoon. Breathe in the yummy chai smells.

In a medium pot, combine the smashed ingredients with the pepper, black tea and water. Cover and bring to a boil. Simmer, covered, for 10 to 15 minutes. Strain through a fine tea sieve. Store in a sealed container in the fridge for 3 to 4 days.

Almond Chai

Makes 1 cup

Brewing your own chai concentrate is easier than it sounds. To determine what works for you, we recommend experimenting with the ratios in the Chai Concentrate recipe (page 243). You can also make a speedy version by steeping 4 tablespoons loose-leaf chai tea or 4 chai tea bags in 1 cup boiling water for 10 to 20 minutes. It won't be exactly the same, but it will still be delicious.

½ cup Almond Milk (page 219) or other non-dairy milk

½ cup Chai Concentrate (page 243) or store-bought

1 teaspoon pure maple syrup (or to taste)

1 stick cinnamon or pinch of ground cinnamon, for garnish

Whisk together the Almond Milk, Chai Concentrate and maple syrup.

For an iced chai, serve over ice or in a tall chilled glass with a dash of ground cinnamon.

For a hot chai latté, heat the mixture in a small pot, whisking to combine. Turn off heat just before it reaches a boil (boiling will hurt the texture). Serve in a mug with a cinnamon stick.

Seal in an airtight container in the fridge for up to 3 days.

VARIATION

RICH CHAI / If you are drinking your chai warm, consider melting ¼ to ½ teaspoon coconut oil into the mixture while it simmers. This is particularly recommended if you are not using our Almond Milk (page 219), which includes coconut oil. Fats help to bring out the flavours of the chai spices. This makes for a rich, layered, satiating treat. Add ¼ teaspoon vanilla extract for additional excitement.

DIRTY CHAI / In café speak, a dirty chai is usually a chai latté with a shot of espresso thrown in. It may sound a bit odd, and it is, but we really like it.

For a cold dirty chai, combine 1 cup chilled Almond Chai with 4 tablespoons Cold-Brew Coffee (page 242). Serve in a tall chilled glass or over ice with a sprinkle of cinnamon.

For a hot dirty chai, add 1 espresso shot or 4 tablespoons hot-brewed coffee to 1 cup warmed-up Almond Chai. Serve in a mug with a cinnamon stick.

Tonics

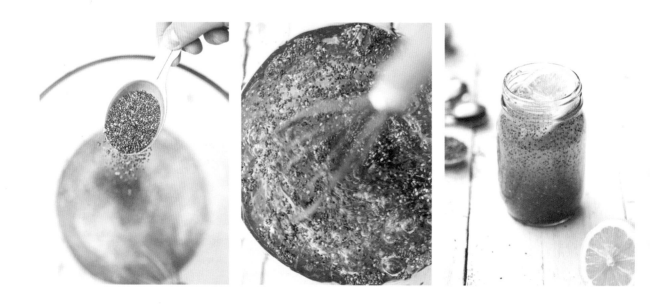

Chia Seed Hydrator

Makes about 2 cups

This is a textural experience. The base is akin to mild lemonade, but the strangely bubble tea–like chia seeds are undoubtedly the main attraction. A complete protein and an excellent source of fibre and omega-3s, these hard-working little seeds are energizing, filling and great for digestion. When you soak them in water, they begin to sprout, which makes their nutrients more bioavailable. The texture may take some getting used to, but it's worth it. This tonic is great for after a workout—and whisking up a batch counts as a workout!

2 cups filtered water

1 tablespoon freshly squeezed lemon juice

½ tablespoon pure maple syrup (optional; see variation)

1 tablespoon chia seeds

In a bowl, whisk together the water, lemon juice, maple syrup (if using) and chia seeds for about 2 minutes or until the chia seeds have started absorbing the water and acquire a clear layer around them. When this happens, it means that they have begun to sprout. If you don't whisk enough they'll clump together and sink to the bottom.

Once the seeds have taken on a bubble tea–like texture and begun to float as if suspended, your hydrator is ready. Serve chilled. Store in an airtight container in the fridge for up to 1 week.

VARIATION

UNSWEETENED CHIA / Omit the maple syrup if you're avoiding sugars or if you are drinking this as part of our Green Cleanse (page 279).

Clean-Zing

Makes about 2¼ cups

This one is cleansing. It is also clean with a zing. Hence the utterly ingenious (and deeply confusing) name. You've probably heard that a squeeze of lemon in warm water first thing in the morning is a great way to get your system going. The cayenne kicks it up a notch here, waking up your metabolism (and the rest of you). If you have access to liquid cayenne (which can be found at some health food stores or online), it offers a more even distribution. If you're using the powdered variety, just be careful to stir well before drinking so you don't get it all in one fiery sip. We make a hot mug of this first thing most mornings.

2 cups filtered hot or cold water

¼ cup freshly squeezed lemon juice

1 tablespoon pure maple syrup (optional; see variation)

¼ teaspoon ground cayenne pepper or liquid cayenne (more to taste)

In a mason jar, pitcher or thermos, combine the water (near boiling for a hot version and room temperature or cold for a cold version), lemon juice, maple syrup (if using) and cayenne. Shake or stir well until combined. Taste for spice and add another pinch of cayenne if desired.

Serve in a mug or glass with a spoon or stirring device. Stir before each sip to ensure the cayenne is evenly distributed. Store in an airtight container in the fridge for up to 2 weeks.

VARIATION

UNSWEETENED CLEAN-ZING / Omit the maple syrup if you're avoiding sugars or if you are drinking this as part of our Green Cleanse (page 279).

Hydra

Makes about 2 cups

Hydra is a Greek island. There are no cars on the island; surefooted donkeys carry tourists' luggage through the narrow, sloping alleys that wind from the port and lead to clusters of whitewashed houses. Pronounced "hee-drah," not "high-drah," it's not to be confused with the mythological beast that had Hercules up in arms. Though it's not quite as relaxing as a trip to the island, in its modest way, this cooling tonic offers a moment of calm in your day. Its cucumber will help your skin stay radiant, and its ginseng, a stimulating herb that you can find in tincture form at most health food stores or online, will help you focus your imagination on the task at hand, whatever that may be.

¼ cucumber, unpeeled, coarsely chopped

4 sprigs parsley

½ lemon, peeled, white pith intact

1½ cups filtered water

¼ teaspoon ginseng (we use Chinese Siberian ginseng in tincture form, and the recommended dose is 1 mL, or roughly ¼ teaspoon or 30 drops; follow the dosage instructions on your bottle)

You'll need a juicer for this one. Run the cucumber, parsley and lemon through the juicer into a jar. We find that juicing the parsley in between the cucumber and lemon helps to extract the most juice possible.

Add the water and ginseng drops. Stir to combine. Taste and adjust if necessary. Serve chilled.

PRO TIP

Don't drink this one right before bed. Ginseng is a mild natural stimulant.

Teresa's Ginger Drink

Makes 4 cups

Our friend Teresa Ayson has been a huge part of Greenhouse's life. She has generously devoted herself to the company for stints at a time, initially when we were juicing out of our first little shop, and again with the writing of this book—not to mention her continuous doses of moral support, enhanced by soups made from vegetables she grows in her garden. While no one makes this tonic quite as well as Teresa, we highly recommend you try; even an imperfect batch is better than most other things.

4 cups filtered water

1 cup peeled and grated fresh ginger (roughly 3 full knobs: see pro tip)

1 cup pure maple syrup or honey

1½ cups freshly squeezed lemon juice (about 9 to 10 lemons)

Boil the water, then add the ginger (grated or prepared according to the pro tip below) and hot water into a large mixing bowl and combine. While this mixture is still warm, add the maple syrup or honey and stir with a wooden spoon until it has fully melted into the water. Let the mixture cool, then strain it once through a mesh sieve. Add the lemon juice to the ginger–maple syrup mixture.

This makes a concentrated tonic. Dilute with water (hot or cold) to taste. Drink warm in winter and over ice in summer. Store in a sealed container in the fridge for up to 2 weeks.

PRO TIP

Prepare your ginger by chopping off the ends and peeling it; peel it entirely if the skin is thick and leathery, or just by scraping off any dark spots with a sharp paring knife if the skin is fine and papery. Cut it into 2- to 3-inch pieces. Wash these.

Blend the ginger pieces with a big splash of warm water until you get a pulp/mulch. Make sure all of the chunks get pulverized. If you don't have a blender, coarsely grate the ginger with a standing cheese grater.

VARIATION

MINTY LEMON GINGER DRINK / Dilute with fresh mint tea instead of water, or add shredded fresh mint leaves at the end.

YYZ

This is our pre-travel tonic. Turmeric and ginger are potent anti-inflammatories that help keep your joints from getting stiff on a long flight. Ginger also enhances your immune system, boosts circulation and helps to ease nausea, while camu camu is a rich source of vitamin C. Turmeric is a bit soapy-tasting on its own, and a shot of straight ginger tastes like breathing fire; diluting them in some freshly squeezed orange juice is a good way to make them more palatable. We like to drink this as a shot, but don't hesitate to increase the orange juice ratio or use a different juice as the base.

2 teaspoons turmeric
juice (1-inch piece)

2 teaspoons ginger
juice (1-inch piece)

1 tablespoon freshly squeezed
orange juice, or to taste

¼ teaspoon camu camu berry
powder

Combine the turmeric juice, ginger juice, orange juice and camu camu berry powder in a glass and stir to combine. Store in a sealed container in the fridge and drink within 3 days.

Beet Kvass

Makes about 3 cups

Kvass is as much fun to make as it is to say. A non-alcoholic fermented drink that has been a Slavic and Baltic staple for generations, kvass originated as early as the Middle Ages, when it evolved as a safe alternative to contaminated water. (In other parts of the world, people were quenching their thirst while avoiding disease with alcoholic beer and wine.) It is traditionally made from stale rye bread, but here we make it from antioxidant-rich red and golden beets. Though it is something of an acquired taste, this is an excellent blood tonic, liver cleanser and digestion regulator. Serve it very cold and drink a small cup at a time.

1 red beet, trimmed and chopped into 1-inch cubes

1 golden beet, trimmed and chopped into 1-inch cubes

2-inch piece fresh ginger, peeled and coarsely chopped

1 teaspoon sea salt

1½ tablespoons pure maple syrup

3 cups filtered water

Place the chopped beets, chopped ginger, salt and maple syrup in a sanitized 1-quart jar. The chopped beets and ginger should take up approximately the bottom half of the container. Add the water to bring the volume up to an inch or so below the jar's top. Don't add more water than that—a little less than 3 cups water is fine too. Seal the jar with a lid and shake it around a bit to evenly disperse the ingredients.

Leave the jar at room temperature for 3 to 7 days. (Climate affects the rate of fermentation; in a hotter, more humid environment, 3 days should be sufficient; in winter, a week or more may be necessary.)

Every day or every other day, "burp" your kvass; that is, let a little gas escape from the lid so that it doesn't explode. Don't worry if you see a little film develop on the top of your kvass during the fermentation process. This is completely normal. Just scoop it out with a spoon.

Your kvass is ready to drink when it has a pleasantly sour, earthy flavour. Strain out the beets and ginger and refrigerate. Serve very cold. It will stay good for several weeks or even a few months. Avoid contamination; don't drink directly from the jar and handle with clean hands.

Nettle Switchel

Makes just over 4 cups

"I will give a traveler a cup of switchel, if he want it; but am I bound to supply him with a sweet taste?" pondered Herman Melville in his 1856 comedic sketch "I and My Chimney." Made properly, switchel indeed does not supply a sweet taste. A traditional quencher sometimes referred to as haymaker's punch because of its alleged popularity among 19th-century American farmers during hay harvest time, switchel should be tart, sour and refreshing. Switchel is usually made with water as its base, but here we have upgraded it with light, herbal-tasting nettle tea.

4 cups filtered water

4 tablespoons dried nettle leaves or 3 to 4 nettle tea bags (see pro tip)

4 tablespoons apple cider vinegar

4 teaspoons pure maple syrup

4 to 8 teaspoons grated fresh ginger or 2 to 4 tablespoons ginger juice

Boil the water, and remove it from heat. Place the nettle leaves in the water, cover and steep for at least 1 hour, or overnight (the longer the better). Strain and discard the nettle leaves.

Pour the nettle tea into a clean 1-quart jar, then add apple cider vinegar, maple syrup and grated ginger or ginger juice (to taste). Let the flavours combine for at least 30 minutes at room temperature, or up to several days in the fridge. If you're using grated ginger, the longer you let it infuse, the more gingery your switchel will be.

When you're ready to serve your chilled switchel, strain it into glasses through a tea sieve. Serve over ice. It will keep well in a sealed jar in the fridge for several weeks.

PRO TIP

Though nettles sting your skin when you meet them in the wild, drinking tea made from their dried leaves (which you can find at health food stores) has diuretic and kidney-cleansing properties, helps to maintain healthy skin and may even offer relief from premenstrual cramps. A word of warning: Nettles are a medicinal plant and are not ideal for everyone. If you have low blood pressure or low blood sugar or are in the early stages of a pregnancy, replace the nettle tea with water.

Healing Vegetable Broth

Makes 10 to 12 cups

Bone broth has received a great deal of attention lately, and understandably so; there's nothing quite as comforting as a steaming, flavourful mug of broth on a cold day. We set out to create a plant-based alternative that would be just as restorative. Made from fermented soybeans, miso contains beneficial minerals, enzymes and healthy bacteria. There are many different varieties of miso, each with its own colour and taste; dark brown miso is often stronger thanks to a longer fermentation period, and light miso is a good place to start if you're relatively new to the flavour. You can serve this broth on its own in a mug, in a small bowl with some chopped green onion and tofu.

10 to 12 cups filtered water

1 medium onion, halved

4 cloves garlic, halved

2-inch piece fresh ginger, halved

2-inch piece fresh turmeric, halved

2 stalks celery, halved

4 carrots, halved

1 tablespoon apple cider vinegar

1 piece kombu seaweed

Any vegetable, ginger and turmeric fibre you have on hand (see pro tip)

3 tablespoons light or dark miso paste

Salt and pepper, to taste

In a large soup pot, combine the water, onion, garlic, ginger, turmeric, celery, carrots, apple cider vinegar, kombu and vegetable fibre. Bring to a boil and allow to boil on high for 1 to 2 minutes. Reduce heat and simmer, covered, for 6 to 12 hours.

Once it has taken on the rich flavours of your ingredients and is golden brown, remove the broth from the heat and strain out the solids. Now add the miso. It's important not to add it earlier, as boiling the miso will denature its beneficial enzymes and kill off its healthy bacteria, which are good for your gut.

Add salt and pepper to taste after straining, but be warned that miso is salty, so you shouldn't need much salt (if any). Serve the broth on its own, or use to cook rice or quinoa or as a base for soup. Store in a sealed container in the fridge or freezer.

PRO TIP

This is a great way to use the pulp from all of your vegetable juices. Leftover fibre from juicing beets, squash, carrots, celery, green vegetables, turmeric and ginger (though be careful with quantities of the last two, as they are potent) are all excellent additions to this warming winter tonic. If you are planning to reserve ingredients for the broth, juice your fruits and your vegetables separately; fruit pulp may add an unwelcome sweetness to this savoury broth.

Cleanses

What Is a Cleanse?

With the cool, sunny mornings of early springtime comes an annual ritual: spring cleaning. Many of us prepare our homes for the season of rebirth by streamlining and making room for greater efficiency. We rid our closets of insulating clutter and scrub their innermost corners with meticulous vigour. We shed the layers beneath which we had cocooned ourselves for the sluggish winter months and rediscover the tingling that comes with starting afresh. There is a bodily version of this, though it is not everyone's cup of tea. It's called a juice cleanse.

The best way to approach a juice cleanse is in three phases: pre-cleanse, cleanse and post-cleanse. The pre- and post-cleanse periods should involve several days of eating a predominantly plant-based diet that includes an abundance of raw and preferably organic vegetable juices, and is free of alcohol, caffeine, sugar and refined or processed foods. It sounds draconian, we know, but the more care you devote to easing yourself into and out of a cleanse, the deeper and longer-lasting its positive effects will be. For many of us, the pre-cleanse period is enough of a reset in and of itself; living like this for two weeks is a wonderful way to break bad habits and wipe the slate clean.

The intervening cleanse phase entails drinking only organic vegetable and fruit juices and nut milks for a short period, typically between one and three days. If you're trying this for the first time, take it slow. Start with three days of pre-cleansing, and if you feel ready, try a one-day juice cleanse. We have included three cleanse guides in this section—the Gentle Cleanse, the Standard Cleanse and the Green Cleanse—based on recipes from this book. We have also included our answers to some frequently asked questions. We worked with our team of in-house nutritionists to develop these programs, but we are not doctors. Please treat the guides and our answers as outlines, not as rules. Everyone is different, and the most important thing is to listen to your body, pay attention to its needs and do what feels right for you.

Cleanse FAQs

Can anyone cleanse?

We don't believe that cleansing is ideal for everyone. If you have a medical condition, are on prescription medication or have any doubts about whether cleansing would be safe for you, we strongly advise that you speak with your doctor. We do not recommend cleansing if you are pregnant, breastfeeding or under 18 years of age.

Is cleansing the only way to truly benefit from juice?

Absolutely not! As you're probably sick of hearing by now, we're big advocates of what we call recreational juicing. Replacing your afternoon coffee or sugary snack with a green juice is a sustainable way to integrate the benefits of juicing into your life.

Is cleansing a "quick fix"?

Unfortunately, there is no such thing as a quick fix in the nutrition world; day-to-day habits are the most important determinant of long-term results. If you enter a cleanse with the mindset that it's a quick, isolated event that will result in long-term magic, it may well prove disappointing. You might lose a few pounds, but if you go straight back to your previous habits after the cleanse, you will likely gain them back.

Instead of viewing a cleanse as a quick fix, we recommend looking at it as a way to instigate positive changes that will result in long-term benefits. Cleansing allows us to take stock of what we put into our bodies and how it makes us feel. This can lead to conquering cravings and making wiser nutritional choices, which can help us look and feel our best in the long term.

Can I work while cleansing?

There is a common misconception that you will spend the duration of your cleanse sprawled on a settee with cucumber slices over your eyes. This should not be the case. If you prepare yourself properly and ease into it, you should be able to go about your normal life. However, do schedule your cleanse at a time when you can listen to your body's needs and follow them. Your busiest and most stressful week of the year would not be the ideal time for a cleanse! You will need to get plenty of sleep.

Can I drink water while cleansing?

Yes. Staying hydrated while cleansing is extremely important. You should drink water before and between each of your juices.

What about herbal tea?

Yes, we recommend drinking herbal tea throughout the day. This is especially advisable if it is chilly outside. You may find that cleansing causes your inner thermometer to drop, and it's important to keep yourself warm. If you feel yourself getting chilly, we recommend wearing an extra layer and/or a scarf throughout your cleanse.

The following teas can be helpful while cleansing:

- Lemon: Supports the immune system
- Ginger: Soothes the stomach, supports the immune system and warms the body
- Hibiscus: Supports blood sugar levels
- Rosehip: High in vitamin C
- Dandelion root: Supports detoxification
- Marshmallow root: Soothing to the intestines

Can I exercise while cleansing?

It is important to keep moving while you are cleansing, but take it easy. Try replacing high-intensity cardio with a power walk, a swim or a gentle yoga class.

What about fibre?

It is very important to get enough fibre while cleansing to make sure you're having daily bowel movements. We always include a Chia Seed Hydrator (page 249) in our cleanse guides, because chia seeds contain both soluble and insoluble fibre (as well as being a complete protein) and are helpful with elimination. You may require extra fibre while cleansing; approximately 2 to 3 tablespoons should do the trick.

How should I transition out of the cleanse?

You should ease out of your cleanse in the same way that you eased into it. That means keeping processed foods, refined flour and sugar, alcohol, caffeine, dairy and meat out of your diet for at least the first few days, and prioritizing vegetables, fruits, pulses, whole grains and nuts. Your first few meals should be small and easy to digest. Eat slowly and chew carefully. Drink lots of water and continue drinking one to three juices per day.

Pre- and Post-Cleanse Menus

Juices

The Good (page 153)
East of Eden (page 154)
The Giver (page 165)
8½ (page 182)
Oz (page 170)
TKO (page 181)
Ophelia (page 177)
Deep Roots (page 161)
Boom (page 174)
Rabbit, Run (page 162)

Breakfasts

Leo (page 194)
Radio (page 205)
Wild Oats (page 209)
Picante Green (page 193)
Firefly (page 201)
Dark Cherry Berry Smoothie Bowl (page 31)
Peach Crisp Smoothie Bowl (page 32)
Avocado Toast with Harissa and Sprouts (page 50)
Moroccan Sweet Potato Hash (page 53)
Warming Winter Oatmeal with Roasted Chestnut Purée (page 40)

Lunches

Pea Shoot and Asparagus Salad with Toasted Hazelnuts (page 57)
Kale Salad with Roasted Beets and Avocado (page 58)
Broccoli Soup with Sweet Potato Croutons (page 61)
Tuscan White Bean Soup with Dinosaur Kale (page 65)
Socca with Walnut Pesto and Arugula (page 66)
Warm Beet Hummus (page 99) with Ancient Grain, Seed and Nut Loaf (page 46)

Dinners

Quinoa Pilaf "Chicoutimi" with Peas, Napa Cabbage and Mint (page 69)
Lentils and Brown Rice with Rainbow Chard, Roasted Carrots and Tahini (page 79)
Spaghetti Squash with Ginger, Chili, Lime and Grilled Tofu (page 70)
Very Veggie Curry with Exploded Yellow Lentils (page 87)
Summer Ratatouille with Creamy Polenta (page 74)
Soba Noodles in Miso Broth with Daikon, Mushrooms and Crispy Tofu (page 85)

Bites

Naked Almonds (page 120)
Baked Brassica Bites (page 115)
Warm Beet Hummus (page 99)
Raw Carrot Chipotle Dip (page 104)
Flax Crackers with Black Olives (page 108)

Gentle Cleanse

—————

Also known as the boyfriend cleanse, this easygoing detox will not leave
you wanting to gnaw on your loafers. It's perfect for a first-timer.

1. First thing

2 cups Wake Up (page 158)

2. Mid-morning

1 cup Almond Milk, made with half the dates (page 219)

3. Around noon

2 cups East of Eden (page 154)

4. Mid-afternoon

1 cup Brazil Nut Milk (page 224)

5. Late afternoon

2 cups The Good (page 153), The Giver (page 165),
TKO (page 181) or 8½ (page 182)

6. After work

2 cups Deep Roots (page 161) or Boom (page 174),
with 1 serving YYZ (page 257)

7. Evening

2 cups Chia Seed Hydrator (page 249)

Standard Cleanse

———

This is our classic cleanse. Striking a delicate balance between wellness and pleasure, it is suitable for all levels of curiosity and experience.

1. First thing

2 cups Clean-Zing (page 250)

2. Mid-morning

2 cups East of Eden (page 154)

3. Sip throughout the day

2 cups Brazil Nut Milk, made with half or no dates (page 224)

4. Early afternoon

2 cups The Good (page 153), 8½ (page 182) or The Giver (page 165)

5. Late afternoon

1 serving YYZ (page 257)

6. After work

2 cups Deep Roots (page 161) or Boom (page 174)

7. Evening

2 cups Chia Seed Hydrator (page 249)

Green Cleanse

With no sweet fruits or sugars of any kind, this is our most rigorous cleanse,
suitable for green juice fans and intermediate to advanced cleansers.

1. First thing

2 cups Clean-Zing, made with no maple syrup (page 250)

2. Mid-morning

2 cups The Good (page 153)

3. Sip throughout the day

2 cups Brazil Nut Milk, made with no dates (page 224)

4. Early afternoon

2 cups The Giver (page 165)

5. Late afternoon

1 serving YYZ (page 257)

6. After work

2 cups 8½ (page 182) or TKO (page 181)

7. Evening

2 cups Chia Seed Hydrator, made with no maple syrup (page 249)

Acknowledgements

There are many people without whom this book would not have been possible. We'd like to thank Rick Broadhead, our fearless agent, and Andrea Magyar, our editor at Penguin Random House, for their unending patience and support.

We are also deeply indebted to Don and Denyse Green for allowing us to test and shoot all of these recipes in their kitchen using every pot, pan, spoon, tablecloth and bowl they own, and for providing invaluable inspiration and feedback throughout the process. Without their generosity, cookware, tableware and decades of trailblazing in the realm of health and wellness, this book could not exist.

For their guidance, moral support and tactfully delivered feedback we'd like to thank Colleen Flood, Douglas Knight, John Plunkett, Shelley Ambrose, Heather Reisman, Sarah MacLachlan, Monica Ainley, Marc de la Villardière, Sophie Green, Matt Kliegman, Christina Gordon and Katharine O'Reilly.

For their recipe contributions, we'd like to thank Alan Bekerman, Brooke Lundmark, Ali Cherniak, Christine Flynn, Colleen Flood, Dean Lane, Denyse Green, Douglas Knight, Elena Mari, Emily Kreeft, Fallon Collett, Jermaine Jonas, Kelly Tyson, Tara Tomulka and Teresa Ayson.

For their help with recipe testing, we'd like to thank Brooke Bunston, Bo Hong, Elizabeth Squibb, Annika Junkin, Tara Tomulka, Ellie Metrick, Katie Schipper, Kelly Tyson, Diane Bald and Alex Budman.

For making life more beautiful, more fun, and a great deal calmer, we'd like to thank Greenhouse Design Director Sarah Dobson.

For her work in putting together the A–Z list of plants and their health benefits, we'd like to thank Jessica Lam.

Finally, I would like to thank the best team in the world: Deeva Green, Lee Reitelman, Elena Mari, Nathan Legiehn, Hana James and my partner in crime (as well as in juice), Anthony Green.

References

Apples

Espley, R.V., C. Brendolise, D. Chagné, S. Kutty-Amma, S. Green, R. Volz, J. Putterill, et al. "Multiple Repeats of a Promoter Segment Causes Transcription Factor Autoregulation in Red Apples." *The Plant Cell* 21, no. 1 (2009): 168–83, doi:10.1105/tpc.108.059329.

Beets

Delgado-Vargas, F., A.R. Jimenez, and O. Paredes-Lopez. "Natural Pigments: Carotenoids, Anthocyanins, and Betalains—Characteristics, Biosynthesis, Processing and Stability." *Reviews in Food Science and Nutrition* 40, no. 3 (2000): 173–289.

Duthie, G.G., S. J. Duthie, J. A. Kyle. "Plant Polyphenols in Cancer and Heart Disease: Implications as Nutritional Antioxidants." *Nutrition Research Reviews* 13, no. 1 (2000): 79–106, doi: 10.1079/095442200108729016.

Ravichandran, K., A.R. Ahmed, D. Knorr, and I. Smetanska. "The Effect of Different Processing Methods on Phenolic Acid Content and Antioxidant Activity of Red Beet." *Food Research International* 48, no. 1 (2012): 16–20, doi:10.1016/j.foodres.2012.01.011.

Blue-Green Algae

Capelli, B., and G.R. Cysewski. "Potential Health Benefits of Spirulina Microalgae: A Review of the Existing Literature." *Nutrafoods* 9, no. 2 (2010): 19–26, doi:10.1007/BF03223332.

Butternut Squash

Rahal, A., Mahima, A. K. Verma, A. Kumar, R. Tiwari, S. Kapoor, S. Chakraborty, et al. "Phytonutrients and Nutraceuticals in Vegetables and Their Multi-dimensional Medicinal and Health Benefits for Humans and Their Companion Animals: A Review." *Journal of Biological Sciences* 14, no. 1 (2014): 1–19, doi:10.3923/jbs.2014.1.19.

Cacao Powder

Cádiz-Gurrea, M.L., J. Lozano-Sanchez, M. Contreras-Gámez, L. Legeai-Mallet, S. Fernández-Arroyo, and A. Segura-Carretero. "Isolation, Comprehensive Characterization and Antioxidant Activities of Theobroma Cacao Extract." *Journal of Functional Foods* 10 (2014): 485–98, doi:10.1016/j.jff.2014.07.016.

Lecumberri, E., R. Mateos, M. Izquierdo-Pulido, P. Rupérez, L. Goya, and L. Bravo. "Dietary Fibre Composition, Antioxidant Capacity and Physico-Chemical Properties of a Fibre-Rich Product from Cocoa (*Theobroma cacao* L.)." *Food Chemistry* 104, no. 3 (2007): 948–54, doi:10.1016/j.foodchem.2006.12.054.

Carrots

Fabiyi, E.F., B.Z. Abubakar, A.T. Yahaya, A.A. Yakubu, and D.H. Yakubu. "Carrot Intake Its Perception, Nutritional Value and Health Benefits: A Case Study of Sokoto Metropolis, Sokoto State, Nigeria." *Pakistan Journal of Nutrition* 14, no. 3 (2015): 136–40.

da Silva Dias, J.D. "Nutritional and Health Benefits of Carrots and Their Seed Extracts." *Food and Nutrition Sciences* 5, no. 22 (2014): 2147–56.

Cayenne Pepper

Delgado-Vargas, F., and O. Paredes-Lopez. *Natural Colorants for Food and Nutraceutical Uses.* Boca Raton, FL: CRC Press, 2003.

Materska, M., and I. Perucka. "Antioxidant Activity of the Main Phenolic Compounds Isolated from Hot Pepper Fruit (*Capsicum annuum* L.)." *Journal of Agricultural and Food Chemistry* 53, no. 5 (2005), 1750–56.

Tundis, R., F. Menichini, M. Bonesi, F. Conforti, G. Statti, F. Menichini, and M.R. Loizzo. "Antioxidant and Hypoglycaemic Activities and Their Relationship to Phytochemicals in *Capsicum annuum* Cultivars during Fruit Development." *LWT—Food Science and Technology* 53, no. 1 (2013): 370–77, doi:10.1016/j.lwt.2013.02.013.

Celery

Dias, J.S. "Nutritional Quality and Health Benefits of Vegetables: A Review." *Food and Nutrition Sciences* 3, no. 10 (2012): 1354–74.

Profir, A.G., and C. Vizireanu. "Evolution of Antioxidant Capacity of Blend Juice Made from Beetroot, Carrot and Celery during Refrigerated Storage." *The Annals of the University of Dunarea De Jos of Galati. Fascicle VI. Food Technology* 37, no. 2 (2013): 93–99.

Chia Seeds

Muñoz, L.A., A. Cobos, O. Diaz, and J.M. Aguilera. "Chia Seed (*Salvia hispanica*): An Ancient Grain and a New Functional Food." *Food Reviews International* 29, no. 4 (2013): 394–408.

Porras-Loaiza, P., M.T. Jiménez-Munguía, M.E. Sosa-Morales, E. Palou, and A. López-Malo. "Physical Properties, Chemical Characterization and Fatty Acid Composition of Mexican Chia (*Salvia hispanica* L.) Seeds." *International Journal of Food Science & Technology* 49, no. 2 (2014): 571–77, doi:10.1111/ijfs.12339.

Coconut Oil

Yeap, S.K., B.K. Beh, N.M. Ali, H.M. Yusof, W.Y. Ho, S.P. Koh, N.B. Alitheen, and K. Long. "Antistress and Antioxidant Effects of Virgin Coconut Oil in Vivo." *Experimental and Therapeutic Medicine* 9, no. 1 (2015): 39–42, doi:10.3892/etm.2014.2045.

Collards

Campos, F.M., J.B.P. Chaves, R.M.C. de Azeredo, D.S. Oliveira, and H.M. Pinheiro Sant'Ana. "Handling Practices to Control Ascorbic Acid and β-Carotene Losses in Collards (*Brassica oleracea*)." *Food Science and Technology International* 15, no. 5 (2009): 445–52.

Franke, A.A., L.J. Custer, C. Arakaki, and S.P. Murphy. "Vitamin C and Flavonoid Levels of Fruits and Vegetables Consumed in Hawaii." *Journal of Food Composition Analysis* 17, no. 1 (2004): 1–35.

Cucumbers

Agatemor, U., O. Nwodo, and C. Anosike. "Anti-Inflammatory Activity of *Cucumis sativus* L." *British Journal of Pharmaceutical Research* 8, no. 2 (2015): 1–8, doi:10.9734/BJPR/2015/19700.

Ji, L., W. Gao, J. Wei, L. Pu, J. Yang, and C. Guo. "In Vivo Antioxidant Properties of Lotus Root and Cucumber: A Pilot Comparative Study in Aged Subjects." *Journal of Nutrition, Health & Aging* 19, no. 7 (2015): 765–70, doi:10.1007/s12603-015-0524-x.

Kumar, D., S. Kumar, J. Singh, R. Narender, B. Vashistha, and N. Singh. "Free Radical Scavenging and Analgesic Activities of *Cucumis sativus* L. Fruit Extract." *Journal of Young Pharmacists: JYP* 2, no. 4 (2010): 365–68, doi:10.4103/0975-1483.71627.

Fennel

Barros, L., A.M. Carvalho, and I.C.F.R. Ferreira. "The Nutritional Composition of Fennel (*Foeniculum vulgare*): Shoots, Leaves, Stems and Inflorescences. *LWT—Food Science and Technology* 43, no. 5 (2010): 814–18, doi:10.1016/j.lwt.2010.01.010.

Tharanath, V., K. Peddanna, Kotaiah, and D.V.S. Gopal. "Flavonoids Isolated from *Foeniculum vulgare* (Fennel) Have Virostatic Efficiency against Bluetongue Virus." *International Journal of Pharmaceutical Sciences Review and Research* 23, no. 1 (2013): 237.

Ginger

Rupasinghe, V., and K. Gunathilake. "Recent Perspectives on the Medicinal Potential of Ginger." *Botanics: Targets and Therapy* 2015 (2015): 55–63, doi:10.2147/BTAT.S68099.

Singletary, K. "Ginger: An Overview of Health Benefits." *Nutrition Today* 45, no. 4 (2010): 171–83, doi:10.1097/NT.0b013e3181ed3543.

Grapefruit

Habauzit, V., M. Verny, D. Milenkovic, N. Barber-Chamoux, A. Mazur, C. Dubray, and C. Morand. "Flavanones Protect from Arterial Stiffness in Postmenopausal Women Consuming Grapefruit Juice for 6 mo: A Randomized, Controlled, Crossover Trial." *American Journal of Clinical Nutrition* 102, no. 1 (2015): 66–74, doi:10.3945/ajcn.114.104646.

Vikram, A., P.R. Jesudhasan, G.K. Jayaprakasha, B.S. Pillai, and B.S. Patil. "Grapefruit Bioactive Limonoids Modulate *E. coli* O157:H7 TTSS and Biofilm." *International Journal of Food Microbiology* 140, no. 2 (2010): 109–16, doi:10.1016/j.ijfoodmicro.2010.04.012.

Honeydews

Lester, G.E. "Antioxidant, Sugar, Mineral, and Phytonutrient Concentrations across Edible Fruit Tissues of Orange-Fleshed Honeydew Melon (*Cucumis melo* L.)." *Journal of Agricultural and Food Chemistry* 56, no. 10 (2008): 3694–98, doi:10.1021/jf8001735.

Jalapeños

Amarowicz, R. "Antioxidant Activity of Peppers." *European Journal of Lipid Science and Technology* 116, no. 3 (2014): 237–39, doi:10.1002/ejlt.201400036.

Liu, Y., and M.G. Nair. "Non-Pungent Functional Food Components in the Water Extracts of Hot Peppers." *Food Chemistry* 122, no. 3 (2010): 731–36, doi:10.1016/j.foodchem.2010.03.045.

Whiting, S., E. Derbyshire, and B.K. Tiwari. "Capsaicinoids and Capsinoids. A Potential Role for Weight Management? A Systematic Review of the Evidence." *Appetite* 59, no. 2 (2012): 341–48, doi:10.1016/j.appet.2012.05.015.

Kale

Armesto, J., J. Carballo, and S. Martínez. "Physicochemical and Phytochemical Properties of Two Phenotypes of Galega Kale (*Brassica oleracea* L. var. *Acephala* cv. Galega)." *Journal of Food Biochemistry* 39, no. 4 (2015): 439–48, doi:10.1111/jfbc.12151.

Ayaz, F.A., R.H. Glew, M. Millson, H.S. Huang, L.T. Chuang, C. Sanz, and S. Hayırlıoglu-Ayaz. "Nutrient Contents of Kale (*Brassica oleraceae* L. var. *Acephala* DC.)." *Food Chemistry* 96, no. 4 (2006): 572–79, doi:10.1016/j.foodchem.2005.03.011.

Lemons

Guimarães, R., L. Barros, J.C.M. Barreira, M.J. Sousa, A.M. Carvalho, and I.C.F.R. Ferreira. "Targeting Excessive Free Radicals with Peels and Juices of Citrus Fruits: Grapefruit, Lemon, Lime and Orange." *Food and Chemical Toxicology* 48, no. 1 (2010): 99–106, doi:10.1016/j.fct.2009.09.022.

Maca

Sandoval, M., N.N. Okuhama, F.M. Angeles, V.V. Melchor, L.A. Condezo, J. Lao, and M.J.S. Miller. "Antioxidant Activity of the Cruciferous Vegetable Maca (*Lepidium meyenii*)." *Food Chemistry* 79, no. 2 (2002): 207–13, doi:10.1016/S0308-8146(02)00133-4.

Pineapples

Aiyegbusi, A.I., O.O. Olabiyi, F.I.O. Duru, C.C. Noronha, and A.O. Okanlawon. "A Comparative Study of the Effects of Bromelain and Fresh Pineapple Juice on the Early Phase of Healing in Acute Crush Achilles Tendon Injury." *Journal of Medicinal Food* 14, no. 4 (2011): 348–52, doi:10.1089/jmf.2010.0078.

Cervo, M.M.C., L.O. Llido, E.B. Barrios, and L.N. Panlasigui. "Effects of Canned Pineapple Consumption on Nutritional Status, Immunomodulation, and Physical Health of Selected School Children." *Journal of Nutrition and Metabolism* 2014 (2014): 1–9, doi:10.1155/2014/861659.

Red Peppers

Deepa, N., C. Kaur, B. Singh, and H.C. Kapoor. "Antioxidant Activity in Some Red Sweet Pepper Cultivars." *Journal of Food Composition and Analysis* 19, no. 6 (2006): 572–78, doi:10.1016/j.jfca.2005.03.005.

Singletary, K. "Red Pepper: Overview of Potential Health Benefits." *Nutrition Today* 46, no. 1 (2011): 33–47, doi:10.1097/NT.0b013e3182076ff2.

Romaine

Thomas, C. "Romaine's Benefits Are Legion." *Orange County Register*, May 16, 2013. http://ww.ocregister.com/articles/romaine-508738-cup-pita.html.

Spinach

Bondonno, C.P., X. Yang, K.D. Croft, M.J. Considine, N.C. Ward, L. Rich, I.B. Puddey, et al. "Flavonoid-Rich Apples and Nitrate-Rich Spinach Augment Nitric Oxide Status and Improve Endothelial Function in Healthy Men and Women: A Randomized Controlled Trial." *Free Radical Biology & Medicine* 52, no. 1 (2012): 95–102, doi:10.1016/j.freeradbiomed.2011.09.028.

Lisiewska, Z., W. Kmiecik, P. Gębczyński, and L. Sobczyńska. "Amino Acid Profile of Raw and As-Eaten Products of Spinach (*Spinacia oleracea* L.)." *Food Chemistry* 126, no. 2 (2011): 460–65, doi:10.1016/j.foodchem.2010.11.015.

Sprouts

Oh, M., and C.B. Rajashekar. "Antioxidant Content of Edible Sprouts: Effects of Environmental Shocks." *Journal of the Science of Food and Agriculture* 89, no. 13 (2009): 2221–27, doi:10.1002/jsfa.3711.

Swiss Chard

Bozokalfa, M.K., B. Yağmur, T.K. Aşçıoğul, and D. Eşiyok, D. "Diversity in Nutritional Composition of Swiss Chard (*Beta vulgaris* subsp. L. var. cicla) Accessions Revealed by Multivariate Analysis." *Plant Genetic Resources* 9, no. 4 (2011): 557–66.

Tomatoes

Friedman, M. "Anticarcinogenic, Cardioprotective, and Other Health Benefits of Tomato Compounds Lycopene, α-Tomatine, and Tomatidine in Pure Form and in Fresh and Processed Tomatoes." *Journal of Agricultural and Food Chemistry* 61, no. 40 (2013): 9534–50.

Turmeric

Singletary, K. "Turmeric: An Overview of Potential Health Benefits." *Nutrition Today* 45, no. 5 (2010): 216–25, doi:10.1097/NT.0b013e3181f1d72c.

Index

8½ (juice), 182

algae, blue-green: about, 22
almond butter
    Rococoa (smoothie), 189
    Wild Oats (smoothie), 209
Almond Chai, 245
Almond Milk, 219
    Almond Chai, 245
    Choco-Maca-Milk, 235
    Green Milk, 231
    Pink Milk, 228
almonds
    about, 22
    Almond Milk, 219
    Ancient Grain, Seed and Nut
        Loaf, 46
    cheesecake crust, 127
    for pie crust, 140
    Raw Dark Chocolate Bars
        with Fig Base, 107
    roasted, 120
    Smoothie Milk, 227
    soaking, 216
Alpha (juice), 178
amaranth seeds: Ancient Grain,
    Seed and Nut Loaf, 46
Amaranth-Stuffed Vine Leaves
    and Fava Purée with
    Onion Condiment, 91–92
Ancient Grain, Seed and Nut
    Loaf, 46
antioxidants: about, 19
apple cider vinegar: Nettle
    Switchel (tonic), 261
Apple Pecan Squares with
    Caramel Sauce, 136
apples
    about, 22, 154
    Deep Roots (juice), 161
    East of Eden (juice), 154
    Fall Fruit Crumble, 132
    Overnight Oats (var.), 35
    Rabbit, Run (juice), 162

apples, dried: Apple Pecan
    Squares with Caramel
    Sauce, 136
arugula: Socca with Walnut
    Pesto and Arugula, 66
asparagus: Pea Shoot and
    Asparagus Salad with
    Toasted Hazelnuts, 57
avocadoes
    Avocado Toast with Harissa
        and Sprouts, 50
    Dark Cherry Berry Smoothie
        Bowl, 31
    Kale Salad with Roasted
        Beets and Avocado, 58
    Key Lime Cups, 144

Baked Brassica Bites, 115
bananas
    Black Seed (smoothie), 206
    Firefly (smoothie), 201
    Jobim (smoothie), 198
    Leo (smoothie), 194
    Overnight Oats (var.), 35
    Peach Crisp Smoothie Bowl,
        32
    Quinoa Banana Pancakes, 36
    Radio (smoothie), 205
    Rio Deal (smoothie), 190
    Rococoa (smoothie), 189
    Wild Oats (smoothie), 209
Barbeque Eggplant, 100
bars see cookies and bars
basil
    8½ (juice), 182
    Walnut Pesto, 66
beans see green beans; white
    beans
beets
    8½ (juice), 182
    about, 22
    Beet Kvass (tonic), 258
    Boom (juice), 174
    Deep Roots (juice), 161

    Kale Salad with Roasted
        Beets and Avocado, 58
    Pink Milk, 228
    Warm Beet Hummus, 99
bell peppers: Preserved
    Rainbow Peppers, 111
berries
    Berry Eclectic (smoothie), 197
    Blueberry Lemon Bites, 123
    Dark Cherry Berry Smoothie
        Bowl, 31
    Raspberry Tart, 128
Bites
    Baked Brassica, 115
    Blueberry Lemon, 123
    Double Cacao Protein, 123
black pepper
    Chai Concentrate, 243
    Mint and Black Pepper
        Savoury Lassi, 213
Black Seed (smoothie), 206
blenders, 17, 151
blueberries
    Berry Eclectic (smoothie), 197
    Blueberry Lemon Bites, 123
    Dark Cherry Berry Smoothie
        Bowl, 31
blueberries, dried: Blueberry
    Lemon Bites, 123
Boom (juice), 174
    Et Tu, Brutus?, 185
Boyfriend Cleanse, 275
Bragg's Liquid Aminos: about, 78
Brazil nut fibre: Spiced Grain-
    Free Granola, 45
Brazil Nut Milk, 224
    Piloto, 241
Brazil nuts
    about, 23
    Brazil Nut Milk, 224
    Chia Seed Chia Energy Bars,
        119
    Smoothie Milk, 227
    soaking, 216

Spiralized Zucchini Mac and
Cheese with Oat Crumb
Crust, 83
"yogurt" (var.), 39
breads
Ancient Grain, Seed and Nut
Loaf, 46
Avocado Toast, 50
Socca with Walnut Pesto and
Arugula, 66
broccoli
8½ (juice), 182
Baked Brassica Bites, 115
Soup, with Sweet Potato
Croutons, 61–63
brownies, sweet potato, 139
Brussels sprouts: Baked
Brassica Bites, 115
buckwheat groats: Ancient
Grain, Seed and Nut Loaf,
46
butternut squash
about, 23
Alpha (juice), 178
Harvest Milk, 232
TKO (juice), 181

cabbage, napa: Quinoa Pilaf
"Chicoutimi" with Peas,
Napa Cabbage and Mint,
69
cabbage, red: Cabbages and
Kings (juice), 169
cacao nibs: Black Seed
(smoothie), 206
cacao powder, see also choco-
late chips/chunks
about, 23
Choco-Maca-Milk, 235
Double Cacao Protein Bites,
123
Radio (smoothie), 205
Raw Dark Chocolate Bars
with Fig Base, 107
Rococoa (smoothie), 189
Vanilla Bean Chia Pudding
(var.), 42
Cake, Sticky Ginger, with Lemon
Sauce, 143

camu camu berry powder
Firefly (smoothie), 201
YYZ (tonic), 257
Caramel Sauce, 136
cardamom
Chai Concentrate, 243
Harvest Milk, 232
Pistachio, Cardamom and
Rose Water Lassi, 210
carrots
about, 23
Boom (juice), 174
Deep Roots (juice), 161
Healing Vegetable Broth,
263
Lentils and Brown Rice with
Rainbow Chard, Roasted
Carrots and Tahini, 79–80
Oz (juice), 170
Rabbit, Run (juice), 162
Raw Carrot Chipotle Dip, 104
Soba Noodles in Miso Broth
with Daikon, Mushrooms
and Crispy Tofu, 85–86
Spaghetti Squash with
Ginger, Chili, Lime and
Grilled Tofu, 70
Tuscan White Bean Soup
with Dinosaur Kale, 65
Cashew Cream, 61
Cashew Milk, 220
Matcha Ginger Milk, 236
Cashew "Yogurt", 39
cashews
Broccoli Soup with Sweet
Potato Croutons, 61
Cashew Milk, 220
Cashew "Yogurt", 39
Combo Nut and Seed Milk,
223
Raspberry Tart, 128
Raw Carrot Chipotle Dip, 104
soaking, 216
Spiralized Zucchini Mac and
Cheese with Oat Crumb
Crust, 83
Vanilla Bean Cheesecake, 127
cauliflower
Baked Brassica Bites, 115

Very Veggie Curry with
Exploded Yellow Lentils,
87–88
cayenne pepper
about, 23
Clean-Zing (tonic), 250
Picante Green (smoothie),
193
Wake Up (juice), 158
celery
8½ (juice), 182
about, 23
Deep Roots (juice), 161
East of Eden (juice), 154
The Giver (juice), 165
The Good (juice), 153
Healing Vegetable Broth,
263
The Misfit (juice), 166
Raw Carrot Chipotle Dip, 104
TKO (juice), 181
Tuscan White Bean Soup
with Dinosaur Kale, 65
centrifugal juicers, 151
Chai Concentrate, 243
Almond Chai, 245
Dirty Chai, 245
Rich Chai, 245
Sweet Potato Chai
(smoothie), 202
chard see rainbow chard; Swiss
chard
Cheesecake, Vanilla Bean, with
Coconut Whipped Cream,
127
cherries: Dark Cherry Berry
Smoothie Bowl, 31
Chestnut Purée, 40
chia seeds
about, 24
Ancient Grain, Seed and Nut
Loaf, 46
Chai Energy Bars, 119
Chia Seed Hydrator (tonic),
249
Overnight Oats, 35
Vanilla Bean Chia Pudding,
42
chickpea flour: socca, 66

chickpeas
dried, preparing, 99
Hot, Crispy, 112
Warm Beet Hummus, 99
chipotle chili flakes: Raw Carrot
Chipotle Dip, 104
Chips, Za'atar Kale, 116
chlorella
about, 22
Berry Eclectic (smoothie), 197
Choco-Maca-Milk, 235
Choco-Mint Milk, 235
chocolate chips/chunks, see
also cacao powder
Chocolate Hemp Peanut
Butter Balls, 147
Oatmeal Chocolate Chip Sea
Salt Cookies, 131
Sweet Potato Brownies, 139
Chocolate Hazelnut Spread, 49
cilantro
Boom (juice), 174
Picante Green (smoothie), 193
cinnamon
Black Seed (smoothie), 206
Chai Concentrate, 243
Harvest Milk, 232
Rio Deal (smoothie), 190
Sweet Potato Chai
(smoothie), 202
Wild Oats (smoothie), 209
Clean-Zing (tonic), 250
cleanses
Gentle, 275
Green, 279
Standard, 276
cleansing
about, 266
and exercise, 270
and fibre, 270
and herbal teas, 270
menus for before and after,
272–73
as "quick fix", 269
and recreational juicing, 269
transitioning out of, 263
and water, 270
who can use, 269
and work, 269

cloves: Chai Concentrate, 243
cocktails see juice cocktails
coconut flakes
Apple Pecan Squares with
Caramel Sauce, 136
Blueberry Lemon Bites, 123
Double Cacao Protein Bites,
123
for pie crust, 140
Spiced Grain-Free Granola
with Brazil Nut Fibre, 45
Coconut Milk, 239
Coconut Whipped Cream,
127, 140
coconut oil
about, 24
Rich Chai, 245
Rio Deal (smoothie), 190
Rococoa (smoothie), 189
coconut water
about, 173
Berry Eclectic (smoothie),
197
Coconut Milk, 239
Harlequin (juice), 173
Leo (smoothie), 194
Picante Green (smoothie),
193
Coconut Whipped Cream, 127,
140
Cold-Brew Coffee, 242
Dirty Chai, 245
Piloto, 241
Rococo-ldBrew (smoothie),
189
cold presses, 150
collards
about, 24
The Giver (juice), 165
Combo Nut and Seed Milk, 223
Harvest Milk, 232
Condiment, Onion, 95
cookies and bars
Chia Seed Chai Energy Bars,
119
Chocolate Hemp Peanut
Butter Balls, 147
Oatmeal Chocolate Chip Sea
Salt, 131

Raw Dark Chocolate Bars
with Fig Base, 135
Scottish Oatcakes, 107
Sweet Potato Brownies, 139
Crackers, Flax, with Black
Olives, 108
Crispy Tempeh, 77
Crispy Tofu, 85–86
Crumble, Fall Fruit, 132
cucumbers
8½ (juice), 182
about, 24
The Giver (juice), 165
Gold Rush (juice), 157
The Good (juice), 153
Hydra (tonic), 253
Oz (juice), 170
Picante Green (smoothie),
193
Curry, Very Veggie, with
Exploded Yellow Lentils,
87–88

Daikon, with Soba Noodles
in Miso Broth, with
Mushrooms and Crispy
Tofu, 85–86
dandelion root tea: about, 270
Dark Cherry Berry Smoothie
Bowl, 31
Dateless Rococoa (smoothie),
189
dates see Medjool dates
Deep Roots (juice), 161
dips and spreads
Chocolate Hazelnut Spread,
49
Fava Purée, 95
Raw Carrot Chipotle Dip, 104
Roasted Eggplant Dip, 100
Sundried Tomato Tapenade,
103
Warm Beet Hummus, 100
Dirty Chai, 245
Dolmades, Amaranth-Stuffed,
91–92
Double Cacao Protein Bites, 123

E3Live: about, 22

East of Eden (juice), 154
  Kale Margarita, 184
eggplants
  Barbequed, 100
  Miso-Glazed, with Kabocha
    Squash and Black Rice, 73
  Roasted, Dip, 100
  Summer Ratatouille with
    Creamy Polenta, 74
  Very Veggie Curry with
    Exploded Yellow Lentils,
    87–88
8½ (juice), 182
Emily's Homemade Gluten-Free
  All-Purpose Flour, 131
Energy Bars, Chia Seed Chai, 119

Fall Fruit Crumble, 132
farinata, 66
Fava Puŕee, 95
fennel
  about, 24
  Ophelia (juice), 177
fibre
  about, 19
  leftover, uses, 263
figs, dried: Raw Dark Chocolate
    Bars with Fig Base, 107
Firefly (smoothie), 201
Flax Crackers with Black Olives,
    108
flax, ground: about, 39
flax seeds
  Ancient Grain, Seed and Nut
    Loaf, 46
  Apple Pecan Squares with
    Caramel Sauce, 136
  Flax Crackers, 108
  Radio (smoothie), 205
flour, homemade gluten-free
    all-purpose, 131
free radicals, 19
fruit: Fall Crumble, 132
fruit, dried: Spiced Grain-Free
    Granola with Brazil Nut
    Fibre, 45

garlic: Healing Vegetable Broth,
    263

Gentle Cleanse, 275
gin: Wake Up Negroni, 184
ginger
  8½ (juice), 182
  about, 24, 236
  Beet Kvass (tonic), 258
  Cabbages and Kings (juice),
    169
  Chai Concentrate, 243
  The Giver (juice), 165
  Gold Rush (juice), 157
  Harvest Milk, 232
  Healing Vegetable Broth, 263
  Leo (smoothie), 194
  Matcha Ginger Milk, 236
  Minty Lemon Ginger Drink
    (tonic), 254
  Nettle Switchel (tonic), 261
  Rabbit, Run (juice), 162
  Rio Deal (smoothie), 190
  South of Eden (juice), 154
  Spaghetti Squash with
    Ginger, Chili, Lime and
    Grilled Tofu, 70
  Teresa's Ginger Drink (tonic),
    254
  TKO (juice), 181
  YYZ (tonic), 257
ginger juice: Dark and Stormy,
    185
ginger tea: about, 270
ginseng
  about, 253
  Hydra (tonic), 253
The Giver (juice), 165
gluten-free flour, 131
Gold Rush (juice), 157
The Good (juice), 153
Granola, Spiced Grain-Free,
    with Brazil Nut Fibre, 45
grapefruit
  about, 25
  Wake Up (juice), 158
grapes, red: The Misfit (juice),
    166
green beans: Spaghetti Squash
    with Ginger, Chili, Lime
    and Grilled Tofu, 70
Green Cleanse, 279

Green Milk, 231
guajillo peppers: Harissa, 50

Hangry Bites, 123
Harissa, 50
Harlequin (juice), 173
Harvest Milk, 232
hazelnuts
  Chocolate Hazelnut Spread,
    49
  toasted, 57
Healing Vegetable Broth, 263
hemp seeds
  Blueberry Lemon Bites, 123
  Chocolate Hemp Peanut
    Butter Balls, 147
  Combo Nut and Seed Milk,
    223
  Dark Cherry Berry Smoothie
    Bowl, 31
  Jobim (smoothie), 198
  Leo (smoothie), 194
  soaking, 216
  Wild Oats (smoothie), 209
hibiscus tea: about, 270
honey
  Minty Lemon Ginger Drink
    (tonic), 254
  Teresa's Ginger Drink (tonic),
    254
honeydew melons
  about, 25
  Ophelia (juice), 177
Hot, Crispy Chickpeas, 112
Hummus, Warm Beet, 99
Hydra (tonic), 253

jalapeño peppers
  about, 25
  Boom (juice), 174
  Oz (juice), 170
Jobim (smoothie), 198
juice cocktails
  Dark and Stormy, 185
  Et Tu, Brutus?, 185
  Kale Margarita, 184
  Wake Up Negroni, 184
juices
  8½, 182

Alpha, 178
Boom, 174
Cabbages and Kings, 169
Deep Roots, 161
East of Eden, 154
The Giver, 165
Gold Rush, 157
The Good, 153
Harlequin, 173
The Misfit, 166
Ophelia, 177
Oz, 170
Rabbit, Run, 162
vs. smoothies, 17
South of Eden, 154
TKO, 181
Wake Up, 158
juicing equipment
blenders, 151
centrifugal juicers, 151
cold presses, 150
masticating juicers, 151
slow juicers, 151

kabocha squash: Miso-Glazed
Eggplant, Kabocha
Squash and Black Rice, 73
kale
about, 25
East of Eden (juice), 154
The Giver (juice), 165
Kale Margarita (juice cock-
tail), 184
Kale Salad with Roasted
Beets and Avocado, 58
TKO (juice), 181
Tuscan White Bean Soup
with Dinosaur Kale, 65
Za'atar Kale Chips, 116
kale, baby: Leo (smoothie), 194
Key Lime Cups, 144
kiwis: Leo (smoothie), 194
Kvass, Beet, 259

lassi
Mint and Black Pepper
Savoury, 213
Pistachio, Cardamom and
Rose Water, 210

leeks
Broccoli Soup with Sweet
Potato Croutons, 61
cleaning, 63
Summer Ratatouille with
Creamy Polenta, 74
lemon juice
Chia Seed Hydrator (tonic),
249
Clean-Zing (tonic), 250
Firefly (smoothie), 201
Lemon Sauce, 143
Mint and Black Pepper
Savoury Lassi, 213
Minty Lemon Ginger Drink
(tonic), 254
Teresa's Ginger Drink (tonic),
254
lemon tea: about, 270
lemons
8½ (juice), 182
about, 25
Boom (juice), 174
Deep Roots (juice), 161
East of Eden (juice), 154
The Giver (juice), 165
Gold Rush (juice), 157
The Good (juice), 153
Hydra (tonic), 253
Lemon Sauce, 143
Ophelia (juice), 177
Oz (juice), 170
peeling, 153
TKO (juice), 181
Wake Up (juice), 158
lentils
and Brown Rice, with
Rainbow Chard, Roasted
Carrots and Tahini, 79–80
Very Veggie Curry with
Exploded Yellow Lentils,
87–88
Leo (smoothie), 194
lime juice
Leo (smoothie), 194
Picante Green (smoothie),
193
limes
Harlequin (juice), 173

Key Lime Cups, 144
The Misfit (juice), 166

maca powder
about, 25, 235
Choco-Maca-Milk, 235
Rococoa (smoothie), 189
mango: Firefly (smoothie), 201
maple syrup
about, 25
Almond Chai, 245
Beet Kvass (tonic), 258
Berry Eclectic (smoothie), 197
Chia Seed Hydrator (tonic),
249
Clean-Zing (tonic), 250
Matcha Ginger Milk, 236
Minty Lemon Ginger Drink
(tonic), 254
Nettle Switchel (tonic), 261
Pistachio, Cardamom and
Rose Water Lassi, 210
Teresa's Ginger Drink (tonic),
254
marshmallow root tea: about, 270
masticating juicers, 151
matcha powder
about, 26
Leo (smoothie), 194
Matcha Ginger Milk, 236
Vanilla Bean Chia Pudding
(var.), 42
Medjool dates
Almond Milk, 219
Black Seed (smoothie), 206
Brazil Nut Milk, 224
Cashew Milk, 220
Cashew "Yogurt", 39
cheesecake crust, 127
Chia Seed Chia Energy Bars,
119
Chocolate Hazelnut Spread,
49
Chocolate Hemp Peanut
Butter Balls, 147
Combo Nut and Seed Milk,
223
Dark Cherry Berry Smoothie
Bowl, 31

Double Cacao Protein Bites, 123

Firefly (smoothie), 201

Overnight Oats, 35

for pie crust, 140

Raw Dark Chocolate Bars with Fig Base, 107

Rio Deal (smoothie), 190

Rococoa (smoothie), 189

Spiced Grain-Free Granola with Brazil Nut Fibre, 45

Sweet Potato Chai (smoothie), 202

milks see nut/seed milks; Smoothie Milk

millet seeds: Ancient Grain, Seed and Nut Loaf, 46

mint

    Black Seed (smoothie), 206

    Mint and Black Pepper Savoury Lassi, 213

    Minty Lemon Ginger Drink (tonic), 254

    Quinoa Pilaf "Chicoutimi" with Peas, Napa Cabbage and Mint, 69

The Misfit (juice), 166

miso paste

    Healing Vegetable Broth, 263

    Miso-Glazed Eggplant, Kabocha Squash and Black Rice, 73

    Soba Noodles in Miso Broth with Mushrooms and Crispy Tofu, 85–86

    Umami Spicy Sauce, 77

Moroccan Sweet Potato Hash, 53

mujaddara and carrots, 79–80

mushrooms

    Quinoa Pilaf "Chicoutimi" with Peas, Napa Cabbage and Mint, 69

    Soba Noodles in Miso Broth with Daikon and Crispy Tofu, 85–86

    Spicy Tacos with Crispy Tempeh, 77–78

Naked Almonds, 120

Napa Cabbage, with Quinoa Pilaf "Chicoutimi", with Peas and Mint, 69

nettle leaves or tea

    about, 261

    Nettle Switchel (tonic), 261

nut/seed milks

    about, 17

    Almond, 219

    Brazil Nut, 224

    Cashew Milk, 220

    Choco-Maca-Milk, 235

    Combo Nut and Seed, 223

    Green Milk, 231

    Harvest Milk, 232

    Matcha Ginger Milk, 236

    Piloto, 241

    Pink Milk, 228

    Smoothie Milk, 227

    storing, 216

nuts, *see also* almonds; Brazil nuts; cashews; chestnuts; hazelnuts; pecans; pistachios; walnuts

    soaking, 216

Oatmeal Chocolate Chip Sea Salt Cookies, 131

oats, rolled

    Ancient Grain, Seed and Nut Loaf, 46

    Blueberry Lemon Bites, 123

    Chia Seed Chia Energy Bars, 119

    crumble topping, 132

    and gluten, 35

    Oatmeal Chocolate Chip Sea Salt Cookies, 131

    Overnight Oats, 35

    Scottish Oatcakes, 107

    Spiralized Zucchini Mac and Cheese with Oat Crumb Crust, 83

    Warming Winter Oatmeal with Roasted Chestnut Purée, 40

    Wild Oats (smoothie), 209

oats, steel-cut: Ancient Grain, Seed and Nut Loaf, 46

okra: Very Veggie Curry with Exploded Yellow Lentils, 87–88

olives, black

    Flax Crackers, 108

    Kale Salad with Roasted Beets and Avocado, 58

olives, Kalamata: Sundried Tomato Tapenade, 103

onions

    Healing Vegetable Broth, 263

    Lentils and Brown Rice with Rainbow Chard, Roasted Carrots and Tahini, 79–80

    Onion Condiment, 95

    Tuscan White Bean Soup with Dinosaur Kale, 65

Ophelia (juice), 177

orange juice

    Jobim (smoothie), 198

    YYZ (tonic), 257

oranges

    Alpha (juice), 178

    Wake Up (juice), 158

Overnight Oats, 35

Oz (juice), 170

Pancakes, Quinoa Banana, 36

parsley: Hydra (tonic), 253

pea shoots

    The Giver (juice), 165

    Pea Shoot and Asparagus Salad with Toasted Hazelnuts, 57

Peach Crisp Smoothie Bowl, 32

Peanut Butter Chocolate Hemp Balls, 147

pears: Fall Fruit Crumble, 132

peas

    Pea Shoot and Asparagus Salad with Toasted Hazelnuts, 57

    Quinoa Pilaf "Chicoutimi" with Peas, Napa Cabbage and Mint, 69

peas, split yellow: Fava Purée, 95

pecans: Apple Pecan Squares with Caramel Sauce, 136

Pecorino: Pea Shoot and
    Asparagus Salad with
    Toasted Hazelnuts (var.),
    57
peppermint extract
    Black Seed (smoothie), 206
    Choco-Mint Milk, 235
peppers *see* bell peppers; black
    pepper; cayenne pepper;
    guajillo peppers; jalapeño
    peppers; red peppers
Pesto, Walnut, 66
Picante Green (smoothie), 193
Pie, Pumpkin, 140
Pilaf, Quinoa, "Chicoutimi" with
    Peas, Napa Cabbage and
    Mint, 69
Piloto, 241
pine nuts: Kale Salad with
    Roasted Beets and
    Avocado, 58
pineapples
    about, 26
    Cabbages and Kings (juice),
        169
    Gold Rush (juice), 157
    Oz (juice), 170
    Picante Green (smoothie),
        193
Pink Milk, 228
pistachios
    Pistachio, Cardamom and
        Rose Water Lassi, 210
    tart crust, 128
Polenta, Creamy, with Summer
    Ratatouille, 74
Preserved Rainbow Peppers,
    111
protein powder: Jobim
    (smoothie), 198
psyllium seed husks
    Ancient Grain, Seed and Nut
        Loaf, 46
    Wild Oats (smoothie), 209
puddings
    Key Lime Cups, 144
    Vanilla Bean Chia, 42
Pumpkin Pie with Coconut
    Whipped Cream, 140

pumpkin purée
    Pumpkin Pie, 140
    Pumpkin Spice (smoothie),
        202
pumpkin seeds
    Ancient Grain, Seed and Nut
        Loaf, 46
    Combo Nut and Seed Milk,
        223
    Flax Crackers, 108
    soaking, 216
    Sweet Potato Chai
        (smoothie), 202
Pumpkin Spice (smoothie), 202

Quinoa Banana Pancakes, 36
Quinoa Pilaf "Chicoutimi" with
    Peas, Napa Cabbage and
    Mint, 69

Rabbit, Run (juice), 162
Radio (smoothie), 205
rainbow chard
    The Giver (juice), 165
    Lentils and Brown Rice with
        Rainbow Chard, Roasted
        Carrots and Tahini, 79–80
    Ophelia (juice), 177
raspberries
    Berry Eclectic (smoothie), 197
    Tart, with Pistachio Crust, 128
Ratatouille with Creamy
    Polenta, 74
Raw Carrot Chipotle Dip, 104
Raw Dark Chocolate Bars with
    Fig Base, 135
red curry paste: Umami Spicy
    Sauce, 77
red peppers
    about, 26
    Alpha (juice), 178
    Preserved Rainbow Peppers,
        111
    Summer Ratatouille with
        Creamy Polenta, 74
rejuvelac: about, 39
rice, black: Miso-Glazed
    Eggplant, Kabocha
    Squash and Black Rice, 73

rice, brown: and Lentils, with
    Rainbow Chard, Roasted
    Carrots and Tahini, 79–80
Rich Chai, 245
Rio Deal (smoothie), 190
Roasted Eggplant Dip, 100
Rococo-ldBrew (smoothie), 189
Rococoa (smoothie), 189
rolled oats *see* oats
romaine
    about, 26
    East of Eden (juice), 154
    The Good (juice), 153
    Harlequin (juice), 173
rosehip tea: about, 270
rose water: Pistachio,
    Cardamom and Rose
    Water Lassi, 210
rum: Dark and Stormy, 185

salad dressings *see* vinaigrettes
salads
    Kale, with Roasted Beets and
        Avocado, 58
    Pea Shoot and Asparagus,
        with Toasted Hazelnuts,
        57
sauces
    Caramel, 136
    Lemon, 143
    Spicy Umami, 77
    Tahini, 80
Scottish Oatcakes, 107
seed milks *see* nut/seed milks
seeds, *see also* amaranth seeds;
    chia seeds; flax seeds;
    hemp seeds; millet seeds;
    pine nuts; psyllium seed
    husks; pumpkin seeds;
    sunflower seeds
    soaking, 216
slow juicers, 151
smoothie bowls
    Dark Cherry Berry, 31
    Overnight Oats, 35
    Peach Crisp, 32
Smoothie Milk, 227
    Black Seed, 206
    Firefly, 201

Jobim, 198
Overnight Oats, 35
Quinoa Banana Pancakes, 36
Radio, 205
Rio Deal, 190
Rococoa, 189
Sweet Potato Chai, 202
Wild Oats, 209
smoothies
about, 17
Berry Eclectic, 197
Black Seed, 206
Dateless Rococoa, 189
Firefly, 201
Jobim, 198
Leo, 194
Mint and Black Pepper
    Savoury Lassi, 213
Picante Green, 193
Pistachio, Cardamom and
    Rose Water Lassi, 210
Pumpkin Spice, 202
Radio, 205
Rio Deal, 190
Rococo-ldBrew, 189
Rococoa, 189
Sweet Potato Chai, 202
Wild Oats, 209
Soba Noodles in Miso Broth
    with Daikon, Mushrooms
    and Crispy Tofu, 85–86
Socca with Walnut Pesto and
    Arugula, 66
soups
    Broccoli, with Sweet Potato
        Croutons, 61–63
    Healing Vegetable Broth,
        263
    Tuscan White Bean, with
        Dinosaur Kale, 65
South of Eden (juice), 154
Spaghetti Squash with Ginger,
    Chili, Lime and Grilled
    Tofu, 70
Spiced Grain-Free Granola with
    Brazil Nut Fibre, 45
Spicy Mushroom Tacos with
    Crispy Tempeh, 77–78
Spicy Umami Sauce, 77

spinach
    8½ (juice), 182
    about, 26
    The Good (juice), 153
    Green Milk, 231
    Harlequin (juice), 173
    Oz (juice), 170
    Picante Green (smoothie),
        193
    Radio (smoothie), 205
    Wild Oats (smoothie), 209
Spiralized Zucchini Mac and
    Cheese with Oat Crumb
    Crust, 83
spirulina
    about, 22
    Berry Eclectic (smoothie), 197
spreads see dips and spreads
sprouts
    about, 27
    Avocado Toast with Harissa
        and Sprouts, 50
    The Giver (juice), 165
squash see butternut squash;
    kabocha squash; spa-
    ghetti squash; zucchini
Standard Cleanse, 276
steel-cut oats see oats
Sticky Ginger Cake with Lemon
    Sauce, 143
strawberries: Berry Eclectic
    (smoothie), 197
sugar: about, 20
Summer Ratatouille with
    Creamy Polenta, 74
Sundried Tomato Tapenade, 103
sunflower seeds
    Ancient Grain, Seed and Nut
        Loaf, 46
    Combo Nut and Seed Milk,
        223
    Flax Crackers, 108
    soaking, 216
    Spiced Grain-Free Granola
        with Brazil Nut Fibre, 45
sunflower sprouts: The Giver
    (juice), 165
sweet potatoes
    Brownies, 139

Chai Smoothie, 202
Croutons, 63
Harvest Milk, 232
Moroccan Hash, 53
Swiss chard: about, 27
Switchel, Nettle, 261

Tacos, Spicy Mushroom, with
    Crispy Tempeh, 77–78
tahini
    Black Seed (smoothie), 206
    sauce, 80
tamari: about, 78
Tart, Raspberry, with Pistachio
    Crust, 128
tea, black: Chai Concentrate,
    243
tea, herbal: and cleanses, 270
Tempeh, Crispy, 77
tequila: Kale Margarita, 184
Teresa's Ginger Drink (tonic),
    254
TKO (juice), 181
tofu
    Crispy, 85–86
    Spaghetti Squash with
        Ginger, Chili, Lime and
        Grilled Tofu, 70
tomatoes
    about, 27
    Boom (juice), 174
    Summer Ratatouille with
        Creamy Polenta, 74
tomatoes, sundried: Tapenade,
    103
tonics
    about, 18
    Beet Kvass, 258
    Chia Seed Hydrator, 249
    Clean-Zing, 250
    Healing Vegetable Broth, 263
    Hydra, 253
    Minty Lemon Ginger Drink,
        254
    Nettle Switchel, 261
    Unsweetened Chia Seed
        Hydrator, 249
    Unsweetened Clean-Zing, 250
    YYZ, 257

turmeric
   about, 27
   Firefly (smoothie), 201
   Healing Vegetable Broth, 263
   South of Eden (juice), 154
   TKO (juice), 181
   YYZ (tonic), 257
Tuscan White Bean Soup with
   Dinosaur Kale, 65

Umami Spicy Sauce, 77
Unsweetened Chia Seed
   Hydrator (tonic), 249
Unsweetened Clean-Zing (tonic),
   250

vanilla beans
   Almond Milk, 219
   Brazil Nut Milk, 224
   Cashew Milk, 220
   Cheesecake, 127
   Chia Pudding, 42
   Combo Nut and Seed Milk,
      223
   Rio Deal (smoothie), 190
   Rococoa (smoothie), 189
   Smoothie Milk, 227
vanilla extract
   Black Seed (smoothie), 206
   Harvest Milk, 232

Pistachio, Cardamom and
   Rose Water Lassi, 210
Wild Oats (smoothie), 209
vegetables, see also specific
   vegetable
   Baked Brassica Bites, 115
   Healing Vegetable Broth,
      263
   leftover fibre from juicing,
      263
   Spaghetti Squash with
      Ginger, Chili, Lime and
      Grilled Tofu, 70
   Summer Ratatouille with
      Creamy Polenta, 74
   Tuscan White Bean Soup
      with Dinosaur Kale, 65
   Very Veggie Curry with
      Exploded Yellow Lentils,
      87–88
vinaigrettes
   olive oil and white wine vin-
      egar, 57
   olive oil, lemon and Dijon, 58
Vine Leaves, Amaranth-Stuffed,
   91–92
vodka: Et Tu, Brutus?, 185

Wake Up (juice), 158
   Wake Up Negroni, 184

Wake Up Negroni (juice cock-
   tail), 184
Walnut Pesto, 66
Warm Beet Hummus, 99
Warming Winter Oatmeal with
   Roasted Chestnut Purée,
   40
white beans: Tuscan Soup with
   Dinosaur Kale, 65
Wild Oats (smoothie), 209

yogurt
   alternative, made with
      cashews, 39
   Mint and Black Pepper
      Savoury Lassi, 213
   Pistachio, Cardamom and
      Rose Water Lassi, 210
YYZ (tonic), 257

Za'atar Kale Chips, 116
zucchini
   about, 27
   Ophelia (juice), 177
   Spiralized, Mac and Cheese
      with Oat Crumb Crust, 83
   Summer Ratatouille with
      Creamy Polenta, 74
   TKO (juice), 181